MW01223969

Drug Therapy and Substance-Related Disorders

Psychiatric Disorders
Drugs and Psychology for the Mind and Body

Psychiatric Disorders: Drugs and Psychology for the Mind and Body

Drug Therapy and Substance-Related Disorders

BY JOYCE LIBAL

MASON CREST PUBLISHERS

PHILADELPHIA

Mason Crest Publishers Inc., 370 Reed Road, Broomall, Pennsylvania 19008
(866) MCP-BOOK (toll free); www.masoncrest.com

Copyright © 2004 by Mason Crest Publishers. All rights reserved. No part of this
publication may be reproduced or transmitted in any form or by any means, electronic or
mechanical, including photocopying, recording, taping, or any information storage and
retrieval system, without permission from the publisher.

First Edition, 2004
13 12 11 10 09 08 07 06 05   10 9 8 7 6 5 4 3 2

Library of Congress Cataloging-in-Publication Data

Brinkerhoff, Shirley.
  Drug therapy and substance-related disorders / Shirley Brinkerhoff.
      p. cm. — (Psychiatric disorders)
Summary: Describes the characteristics and drug treatment of disorders related to
substance abuse, including alcoholism and other addictions to legal and illegal drugs.
Includes bibliographical references and index.
  ISBN 1-59084-577-3
  ISBN 1-59084-559-5 (series)
1. Substance abuse—Chemotherapy—Juvenile literature. 2. Substance abuse—
Treatment—Juvenile literature. 3. Teenagers—Drug use—Juvenile literature. [1. Substance
abuse—Treatment. 2. Drug abuse—Treatment. 3. Alcoholism—Treatment.] I. Title. II.
Series.
  RC564.3.B756 2004
  616.86'061—dc21

    2003011271

Design by Lori Holland; Cover design by Benjamin Stewart.
Composition by Bytheway Publishing Services, Binghamton, New York.
Printed in the Hashemite Kingdom of Jordan.

This book is meant to educate and should not be used as an alternative
to appropriate medical care. Its creators have made every effort to
ensure that the information presented is accurate—but it is not intended
to substitute for the help and services of trained professionals.

Picture Credits:
Artville: pp. 63, 66, 93, 111. Autumn Libal: pp. 21, 24, 26, 35, 54, 57. Benjamin Stewart: p.
52. Corbis: pp. 65, 119, 120, 122. Corel: p. 28. Digitavision: pp. 10, 50, 69, 104, 106, 109,
110. Image Source: pp. 78, 88, 112, 114. National Library of Medicine: pp. 30, 32.
PhotoDisc: pp. 12, 16, 33, 40, 42, 58, 83, 84, 86. Stockbyte: pp. 15, 36, 39, 44, 45, 46, 61, 64,
66, 76, 90, 95, 97, 98, 100, 113, 116. The individuals in these images are models, and the
images are for illustrative purposes only.

CONTENTS

INTRODUCTION

by Mary Ann Johnson

Teenagers have reason to be interested in psychiatric disorders and their treatment. Friends, family members, and even teens themselves may experience one of these disorders. Using scenarios adolescents will understand, this series explains various psychiatric disorders and the drugs that treat them.

Diagnosis and treatment of psychiatric disorders in children between six and eighteen years old are well studied and documented in the scientific journals. In 1998, Roberts and colleagues identified and reviewed fifty-two research studies that attempted to identify the overall prevalence of child and adolescent psychiatric disorders. Estimates of prevalence in this review ranged from one percent to nearly 51 percent. Various other studies have reported similar findings. Needless to say, many children and adolescents are suffering from psychiatric disorders and are in need of treatment.

Many children have more than one psychiatric disorder, which complicates their diagnoses and treatment plans. Psychiatric disorders often occur together. For instance, a person with a sleep disorder may also be depressed; a teenager with attention-deficit/hyperactivity disorder (ADHD) may also have a substance-use disorder. In psychiatry, we call this comorbidity. Much research addressing this issue has led to improved diagnosis and treatment.

The most common child and adolescent psychiatric disorders are anxiety disorders, depressive disorders, and ADHD. Sleep disorders, sexual disorders, eating disorders, substance-abuse disorders, and psychotic disorders are also quite common. This series has volumes that address each of these disorders.

Major depressive disorders have been the most commonly diagnosed mood disorders for children and adolescents. Researchers don't agree as to how common mania and bipolar disorder are in children. Some experts believe that manic episodes in children and adolescents are underdiagnosed. Many times, a mood disturbance may co-occur with another psychiatric disorder. For instance, children with ADHD may also be depressed. ADHD is just one psychiatric disorder that is a major health concern for children, adolescents, and adults. Studies of ADHD have reported prevalence rates among children that range from two to 12 percent.

Failure to understand or seek treatment for psychiatric disorders puts children and young adults at risk of developing substance-use disorders. For example, recent research indicates that those with ADHD who were treated with medication were 85 percent less likely to develop a substance-use disorder. Results like these emphasize the importance of timely diagnosis and treatment.

Early diagnosis and treatment may prevent these children from developing further psychological problems. Books like those in this series provide important information, a vital first step toward increased awareness of psychological disorders; knowledge and understanding can shed light on even the most difficult subject. These books should never, however, be viewed as a substitute for professional consultation. Psychiatric testing and an evaluation by a licensed professional are recommended to determine the needs of the child or adolescent and to establish an appropriate treatment plan.

FOREWORD

by Donald Esherick

We live in a society filled with technology—from computers surfing the Internet to automobiles operating on gas and batteries. In the midst of this advanced society, diseases, illnesses, and medical conditions are treated and often cured with the administration of drugs, many of which were unknown thirty years ago. In the United States, we are fortunate to have an agency, the Food and Drug Administration (FDA), which monitors the development of new drugs and then determines whether the new drugs are safe and effective for use in human beings.

When a new drug is developed, a pharmaceutical company usually intends that drug to treat a single disease or family of diseases. The FDA reviews the company's research to determine if the drug is safe for use in the population at large and if it effectively treats the targeted illnesses. When the FDA finds that the drug is safe and effective, it approves the drug for treating that specific disease or condition. This is called the labeled indication.

During the routine use of the drug, the pharmaceutical company and physicians often observe that a drug treats other medical conditions besides what is indicated in the labeling. While the labeling will not include the treatment of the particular condition, a physician can still prescribe the drug to a patient with this disease. This is known as an unlabeled or off-label indication. This series contains information about both the labeled and off-label indications of psychiatric drugs.

I have reviewed the books in this series from the perspective of the pharmaceutical industry and the FDA, specifically focusing on the labeled indications, uses, and known side effects of these drugs. Further information can be found on the FDA's Web page (www.FDA.gov).

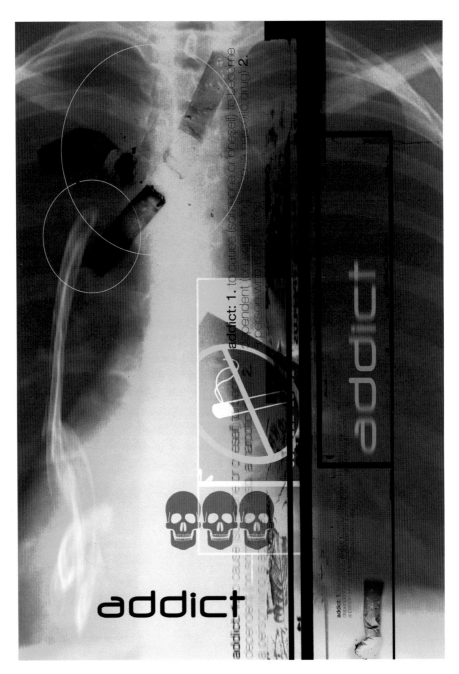

Addiction to drugs or other substances is the cause of substance-related disorders.

1 | Defining the Disorder

If we consider substance-related disorders as a group, they are among the most prevalent of all mental disorders, and every element of society is adversely affected by them. Many different chemicals, both legal and illegal, are involved in substance-related disorders.

The group of Russian dignitaries included medical doctors and others who wanted to improve medical and social care in the former Soviet Union. Aid for International Development had funded their trip to North America where they toured hospitals and social-service agencies. Today they were visiting a recovery facility for teenagers addicted to alcohol.

Although the language being spoken was Russian, admiration for the facility was clear in the voices of these women and men as they strolled across well-manicured lawns and walked through handsome buildings filled with comfortable furniture. The young men playing basketball in the gymnasium looked and acted like typical high school

When a person needs to drink in order to get through her day, she may have a substance-related disorder.

students. Dorm rooms were clean and personal items were stored neatly in proper places. "Keeping your room organized and clean is part of the treatment," explained the counselor leading the tour.

A small group of residents had volunteered to meet with the Russians to answer questions about treatment and the personal journeys that had led each of them to this place. Two translators, who had been flown in from Washington, used whisper microphones to provide their spontaneous translation, which lent an air of importance to the scene. Perhaps it helped everyone realize that understanding substance-induced disorders and successful paths to recovery has global significance.

Of the stories told that afternoon, none affected the visitors more than that of Tom and his gentle fall into an alcoholic abyss. Was Tom lured into dependence on this substance because he became involved with the "wrong crowd" at his high school? Was he abused in some manner that led him to seek relief in bottles of vodka and cans of beer? Did Tom's parents engage in **addictive** behavior that he began to model in his own life? The fact that this handsome, intelligent, courteous adolescent had become a habitual abuser of alcohol puzzled the Russians.

Everyone in the room was attentive as Dr. Solodov posed several questions to Tom through the translator: "Tom, is there anything your parents could have done to prevent this from happening? Were you unhappy about something? Could your mother and father have improved their relationship with you in some way?"

Tom's eyes softened and the hint of a smile crossed his lips. "No." Tom turned his head slowly from side to side. "I have a fantastic family. My dad, he's the best. In fact, he was one of my Boy Scout leaders. Our family did everything together. Dad and I really like to go fishing. We always had great summers and holidays at our cabin on the lake. We had a great relationship until alcohol got in the way. I became an alcoholic. That's what caused the problems in our family.

"There's nothing my family could have done to prevent it. Everything was great. Then my friend Matt and I went to a party at his cousin's house. Matt's cousin went to a high school across town. Matt's aunt and uncle weren't home, and a few of the kids brought beer. I never intended to get drunk, but I didn't know most of the kids at the party, and since most of the kids who were there had a beer in their hands, I decided to just have one and try to join in the conversation. I felt a little less like an outsider with a can of beer like everyone else, I guess. Anyway, I started sipping my beer, and maybe because I wasn't used to drinking, it started to make me feel more relaxed right away. I hadn't talked much until then, but I began to feel less nervous and started to speak up in the conversation. Soon people were

GLOSSARY

addictive: Causing a physical or psychological dependence.

A recognizable pattern exists with the repeated use of many addictive substances that helps to correctly diagnose substance dependence. According to the American Psychiatric Association's *Diagnostic and Statistical Manual of Mental Disorders*, fourth edition, a person need only exhibit three of these in a twelve-month period to be diagnosed with a substance-related disorder.

1. The individual develops tolerance for the substance, meaning that she must ingest more and more of the substance in order to obtain the desired effect.
2. If a person suffering from a substance-related disorder does try to resist the substance, he often experiences a series of unpleasant withdrawal symptoms. These symptoms are usually the opposite of the experiences brought on by the substance. Withdrawal symptoms can lead a person to take more of the substance (or a closely related substance) in order to eliminate the uncomfortable feelings brought on by withdrawal symptoms.
3. It becomes progressively more difficult for the individual to resist consuming the substance, even for one day. In fact, the individual may begin using the substance several times throughout the day. The individual may use the substance for a longer period of time than originally intended and in increasingly larger amounts.
4. The person becomes unable to use a limited amount of the substance even if she has set a limit for herself.
5. Although the individual sincerely wishes to do so, efforts to discontinue use or to decrease the amount of the substance used are unsuccessful.
6. More and more of the person's day may be devoted to the substance (thinking about it, finding ways to acquire it, spending time in areas where it can be used without detection, and actually using it). As a consequence, areas of the person's family and social life might be neglected, as might their employment.
7. Use of the substance continues even if the individual recognizes the negative impact it is having on his well-being, including physical (for example, liver damage caused by alcohol use, malnutrition as a result of heroin use, etc.) as well as psychological problems (for instance, depression following use of cocaine).

talking directly to me, and I was enjoying myself. Before I knew it, the can was empty, and someone asked if I wanted another. Having the can in my hand felt sort of like security and it made me feel older, too, so I said, 'Heck, yeah.' One beer just led to another and another, and that's the story of my addiction really—just one drink leading to another. It all just seemed like fun.

"My parents had gone out that night, so my friends were able to get me into my house and basically dump me off in my bedroom. The next day I stayed in my room until I felt better. My parents never even knew I had gone to a party, and they certainly didn't know I had been drinking. That's the last thing they would have expected of me.

"I hadn't gotten drunk enough to pass out or anything. I was just drunk enough that I was funny, and everybody seemed to really like me. I didn't get terribly sick, although I did have a bear of a headache the next day. Even with the

A person who connects alcohol and good times may not real-ize he has a drinking problem.

headache, though, I remembered the great time I'd had, and I wanted that to happen again. I couldn't remember ever having so many people talk to me or laugh with me. I wanted to go to another party, and when the opportunity presented itself again, I was first in line to have a drink, and then another drink, and another. . . .

"I think I would probably have become an alcoholic no matter when I had taken my first drink. I'm an adventurous person with a curious mind. It wasn't long before I was experimenting with every type of alcohol I could get my hands on. What did it taste like? Did I enjoy drinking it? How many drinks did it take to make me get the feeling I was after?

"My parents kept quite a bit of liquor in the house for business parties. It was after I started sneaking into their supply that Mom first became suspicious and then later re-

Adolescents sometimes begin drinking by raiding their parents' liquor cabinet.

alized what was going on. I didn't want to steal from my parents, but by that time I didn't have a choice—I needed to drink in order to function. When my mom asked me about taking their liquor, I denied it at first, but my parents aren't stupid.

"It wasn't that long before I was hanging one on every weekend. I went on some real benders, coming home drunk and getting sick, so there was no hiding it any longer. My parents tried to control me, but I wasn't controllable by then. They couldn't be with me twenty-four hours a day. I was a very creative drunk. You'd be amazed at the ways I found to get alcohol.

"My parents tried to keep it quiet at first and just handle it in the family. That didn't work, and they eventually talked to my friends. One friend in particular had been getting really worried about me, so he was the first one to tell the truth about my situation. He even helped my parents talk to me about it and about coming here. I was angry at first, but now I'm really grateful to my friend. We've been friends since elementary school. It took a lot of courage to confront me; like I said, he knows me really well, so he realized how angry I'd be with him. I think now we'll be best friends until the day one of us dies."

As human beings, our survival is dependent on eating, drinking, and breathing in order to maintain a healthy body. There are certain classes of substances, however, that interfere with our brain chemistry, bodily functions, and behavior when we eat, drink, smoke, breathe, or inject them. When a person becomes dependent on one of these drugs, medications, or ***toxins***, we describe their condition as a substance-related disorder. When an individual has this type of disorder, he continues to use the substance even though significant behavior or health problems occur as a result of that use.

GLOSSARY

toxins: *Poisonous substances.*

GLOSSARY

lethal: *Having the ability to cause death.*

stimulants: *Substances that speed up biological functions.*

sedatives: *Substances that have a tranquilizing effect, relieve anxiety, calm, and soothe.*

depressants: *Substances that lower the rate of biological functions.*

amphetamine: *A substance that stimulates the central nervous system.*

appetite suppressants: *Chemical substances that lessen the feeling that one must eat.*

over-the-counter drugs: *Medicines available without a prescription.*

A substance-related disorder is characterized by serious and continued negative consequences to habitual use of an addictive substance over a twelve-month period. For example, Tom began to miss school in order to spend more time drinking. His use of alcohol made him physically ill, caused great distress to his parents, and resulted in many family arguments. Yet he continued to drink despite these problems.

Substances with the potential to cause addiction can affect the body physically and mentally. There are so many of these substances that they can be divided into eleven different categories. Some of these chemicals are legal and easily available, while others require a prescription from a physician. Still others are illegal under any circumstances because of their dangerous and potentially **lethal** qualities. Some of the substances act as **stimulants** to the brain and others act as **sedatives** or **depressants**.

With the exception of caffeine, all of these eleven classes of substances have the potential to cause serious substance dependence (some of the common street names for these substances appear in quotation marks).

- Alcohol: a depressant.
- **Amphetamine**, dextroamphetamine, methamphetamine ("speed," "crystal meth"): These are serious stimulants that have a higher potential for abuse. This category also includes substances that have amphetamine-like action such as certain **appetite suppressants**.
- Caffeine: This substance, which is found in coffee, black tea, cocoa, some soft drinks, and many prescription and **over-the-counter drugs**, is considered to be a minor stimulant; it has a lower potential for abuse.

According to the American Psychiatric Association's *Diagnostic and Statistical Manual of Mental Disorders, fourth edition* (the DSM-IV), a person with a substance abuse disorder must demonstrate one or more of the following criteria in a twelve-month period:

1. Recurrent substance use results in failure to meet one's responsibilities at work, school, or home (for example, substance-related absences from school or work; neglect of children or household).

2. Recurrent substance use in situations where it is physically dangerous (for example, while driving a car or operating a machine).

3. Recurrent substance-related legal problems (for example, arrests because of substance-related disorderly conduct).

4. Continued substance use despite social or interpersonal problems (for example, physical fights; arguments with spouse about the consequences of using substances)

GLOSSARY

psychoactive: Having an effect on the mind or behavior.

alkaloid: Found in some plants, this organic substance can have stimulant, toxic, or analgesic qualities.

- Cannabis (marijuana, "pot," "grass," "reefer"): the *psychoactive* ingredient in cannabis is tetra-hydro-cannabinol.
- Cocaine ("crack," "rock," "base," "freebase," "blow"): This is an *alkaloid* derived from coca leaves.
- Hallucinogens (psychedelic drugs): This diverse category includes ergot and related compounds such as

GLOSSARY

paranoia: *A condition characterized by the gradual development of an elaborate pattern of thinking based on the misinterpretation of an event.*

euphoria: *A feeling of well-being or extreme happiness.*

serotonin: *A chemical substance in the brain and blood that affects the transmission of nerve impulses and constriction of blood vessels.*

hypnotics: *Any agents that bring about sleep.*

lysergic acid diethylamide ("LSD," "acid"), phenyl-alkylamines (mescaline, "STP"), methylene dioxymethamphetamine (MDMA, "ecstasy," "X"), indole alkaloids psilocybin ("shrooms"), dimethyltryptamine ("DMT"), and other substances. Psychedelic drugs like LSD and mescaline can have serious and long-lasting effects on the body. Some individuals may experience depression, ***paranoia***, and frightening illusions while using psychedelics on one occasion and then have an opposite experience, including a general feeling of ***euphoria***, the next time. Psychedelics work by affecting ***serotonin*** in the brain.

- Inhalants: Substances such as glue, gasoline, and nitrous oxide are included in this category. Possibly because of easy accessibility of the substances and lack of education on the part of the users, inhalants are most often used by younger people. Inhalants are among the most dangerous substances of abuse as they can kill instantly. Individuals who do survive can suffer permanent damage because brain cells are destroyed by the use of inhalants. Headaches and stomach discomfort are the usual results of use. Most individuals who experiment with inhalants discontinue use as soon as they experience the side effects and understand the extreme risks.
- Nicotine: The addictive ingredient in cigarettes.
- Opioids: morphine, heroin ("smack"), codeine, hydromorphone, methadone, opium, Percodan, oxycodone, meperidine, fentanyl, and medications such as pentazocine and buprenorphine are included in this classification.
- Sedatives, ***hypnotics***, and anxiolytics or antianxiety substances: These include phencyclidine ("PCP," "Angel Dust") or similar acting arylcyclohexylamines,

which may induce ***delirium psychosis***, ***catatonic mutism***, ***coma***, agitation, confusion, or violence. Benzodiazepines, benzodiazepine-like drugs, barbiturates, and barbiturate-like drugs are included in this classification.

Substance-related disorders can be divided into two groups. The first, substance-use disorder, refers to abuse of the substance. When Tom began to use alcohol routinely to feel at ease with other people and when he began experimenting with alcohol to determine his preferences and the amount needed to achieve the effect he desired, he was exhibiting a substance-use disorder.

When Tom became intoxicated on a regular basis and became dependent on alcohol, he had crossed over into the

Alcohol, caffeine, marijuana, and nicotine are all substances that can cause addiction.

GLOSSARY

delirium psychosis: *Mental confusion caused by a psychological disorder.*

catatonic mutism: *An inability to speak due to a psychological condition.*

coma: *A severe disturbance of consciousness in which voluntary activity is diminished or absent.*

second group, substance-induced disorders. This type of disorder can cover a range of situations and behaviors, including intoxication and later withdrawal, both of which Tom experienced. Depending on the substance used, substance-induced disorders can also cause *delirium*, *dementia*, amnesia, *psychosis*, mood disorders, anxiety disorders, sleep disorders, and sexual dysfunction.

Most people who are dependent on addictive substances develop an uncontrollable craving for that substance. Christiane's situation provides another example. When Christiane started taking an occasional cigarette out of her mother's purse so that she could join her friends for "a smoke," one cigarette a week was enough, and her mother was none the wiser. A Saturday-afternoon cigarette smoked in a small clearing in the park was all that was necessary for the group of nine-years-olds to feel grown up. After a time, however, the Saturday cigarette was joined by one and then two other cigarettes, which Christiane smoked in her backyard during the week. Over the years, the number of cigarettes she smoked weekly and then daily continued to escalate. She smoked during several bouts of bronchitis, even though her doctor warned her sternly that she was placing her health in serious jeopardy. Her use of cigarettes was the cause of a breakup with her boyfriend.

By the time Christiane reached her third year of college, she was determined to give up her fifteen-cigarettes-per-day habit. But it certainly wasn't easy. Relapses are common when attempting to control or eliminate use of an addictive substance and recover from a substance-related disorder. Christiane tried several methods and went through many disap-

GLOSSARY

delirium: *Mental confusion that can include hallucinations and a loss of control.*

dementia: *Confusion and loss of memory and intellectual ability.*

psychosis: *A mental disorder characterized by a severely disturbed personality.*

Substance intoxication is often associated with aggressive behavior, criminal activity, accidents, and suicide.

- Intoxicated drivers or pedestrians are involved in approximately one half of all highway fatalities.
- Up to 10 percent of individuals who are dependent on addictive substances commit suicide.

Alcohol Tolerance

Most people who abuse alcohol will develop "tolerance" to alcohol's chemical effects on the body. This means that they have to drink more to get the effect they want emotionally. Many adolescents think they can "hold their liquor" and are proud of their ability to drink so much without acting drunk. They don't realize, though, that this is actually a symptom of alcohol abuse.

pointing relapses before eventually succeeding. She has now been nicotine free for over a year, but she still fights the occasional temptation to light up a cigarette. Because Christiane has not smoked a cigarette in twelve months, she is considered to be in sustained full *remission*.

With the exceptions of nicotine and caffeine, use of any of the remaining classes of substances listed earlier can result in substance intoxication. The symptoms of intoxication can vary, depending on the substance used. When Tom drank a moderate amount of alcohol he became more relaxed and talkative. But as he consumed additional amounts of the substance, his behavior began to change in more negative ways. For example, Tom sometimes lost his balance and spilled his drink, his mood became changeable, and he occasionally acted toward others in a belligerent manner. Even before he drank enough to make himself ill, Tom's thoughts became muddled and his speech was slurred.

All of this happened because the alcohol was affecting Tom's *central nervous system*. People in the medical field can tell when a person has been drinking excessively not

GLOSSARY

remission: A period when something is stopped either partially or entirely.

central nervous system: The part of the nervous system that consists of the brain and spinal cord and that coordinates the sensory and motor activity of the entire nervous system.

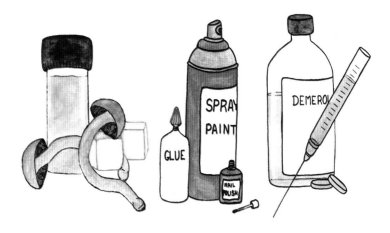

Hallucinogens, inhalants, and opioids are all substances that have a high potential for abuse.

only because they can smell alcohol on the person's breath but also because they can measure it in the person's blood and urine. When an alcohol-induced substance-related disorder becomes more serious, doctors can perform tests on a person's liver to help determine how much physical damage the disorder has caused.

Symptoms exhibited by an individual suffering from a substance-related disorder are dependent on the substance being used, but they are also determined by the person's body chemistry, by the amount of substance used, the duration of use, and other factors. The most common symptoms include impaired thinking, judgment, *perception*, and attention. The person may have difficulty staying awake and experience reduced *psychomotor* ability, or he might have so much energy that he is awake and active all night. The behavior a person exhibits toward others will often be far different than it would be if the substance were not being used.

GLOSSARY

perception: The awareness or understanding of something.

psychomotor: Movement that's directed by mental activity.

When someone who has been using an addictive substance in large amounts for a prolonged period of time tries to discontinue use of the substance, she can experience substance withdrawal. This happens because the individual's brain chemistry has changed in reaction to the substance. If the substance is then not available to the brain, the body reacts in uncomfortable ways. Withdrawal symptoms are often the opposite of the feelings that are brought on by use of an addictive substance.

For example, alcohol is a sedative that depresses the central nervous system. For a person like Tom, withdrawal symptoms begin to develop as the presence of alcohol diminishes in the central nervous system, thus causing the central nervous system to react in a *hyperactive* manner. Tom's withdrawal symptoms (anxiety, sweating, shaking, and rapid heart rate) ended after a few days. Other residents of the facility Tom attended, however, had more prolonged withdrawal symptoms. For example, Tom's friend Bob still had difficulty sleeping several months after discontinuing his use of alcohol. Some individuals can even suffer *seizures* and *hallucinations* during withdrawal from alcohol addiction.

People who successfully conquer withdrawal symptoms and become substance free are said to be in remission. These individuals are extremely vulnerable to temptations to use the substance again during the first twelve months following withdrawal, however, and any use of the substance can reinstate the cycle of dependence.

People with active substance-related disorders often experience many health problems. Tanya began experimenting with a wide variety of substances while she was still in high school. Eventually Tanya tried heroin, and it soon became her drug of choice. One of the major health problems Tanya suffered as a result of her dependence on heroin was

GLOSSARY

hyperactive: Being excessively active.

seizures: Sudden involuntary physical reactions sometimes caused by a chemical imbalance in the body.

hallucinations: Perceptions of objects or sounds that are not real.

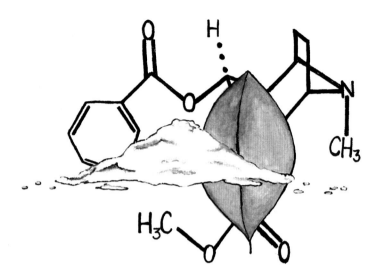

Cocaine is a chemical manufactured from coca leaves.

GLOSSARY

anorexic: *Suffering from an eating disorder characterized by the refusal or inability to maintain a normal weight for age and body type (often by not eating), combined with intense fear of gaining weight.*

malnutrition. That's because Tanya's life became totally dedicated to the pursuit and use of heroin. Obtaining the substance and "shooting up" became the only things Tanya lived for. Family and former friends became insignificant to her, and Tanya didn't care about where she lived or slept; she rarely thought about food. All that mattered to Tanya at the height of her substance-induced disorder was obtaining and injecting more heroin. By the time she sought treatment, Tanya had lost a third of her normal body weight and was seriously *anorexic*.

Physical problems brought on by a substance-related disorder vary depending on the substance used and the physical makeup of the person using the substance. For instance, Greg's use of cocaine caused serious erosion of his nasal passages, while Jane's baby was born with a physiological dependence on cocaine and had to endure withdrawal symptoms as a result of Jane's use of that substance.

The bottom line is that substance-related disorders are dangerous for many reasons. Illegal drugs are, of course, not monitored by any government agency for purity or for dosage. When individuals use these substances, they may be putting *anything* into their bodies. Each usage carries with it the possibility of illness from contaminants as well as overdose from the illegal substance. Very serious medical conditions such as irregular heartbeat; respiratory distress; human immunodeficiency virus (HIV, the virus connected with AIDS), hepatitis, and bacterial infections from contaminated needles can result from continued use of addictive substances.

Some people believe that certain individuals are more susceptible to substance-related disorders, particularly alcoholism, than others because of their genetic makeup. Other evidence suggests that many individuals with a substance-related disorder first used these substances to counteract anxiety or depression; rather than seeking professional help for those conditions, they "self-medicated." In his book *The Essential Guide to Psychiatric Drugs*, Dr. Jack Gorman writes, "Studies have shown that as many as one third of patients undergoing alcohol detoxification had experienced panic attacks before they became alcoholics."

There may be debate about what causes substance-related disorders, but some things are certain. The dangers of addictive substances, the dangers of exposure to other contaminants because of them, and the personal and social toll substance-related disorders cause are reasons why it is essential for individuals with these disorders to seek treatment. If left untreated, substance-related disorders can even be fatal.

Psychiatric medications are among the treatments now available to assist individuals in conquering substance-related disorders.

The early Egyptians may have drunk opium mixed with water as early as 1500 B.C.

2 | Drug History

We would be hard-pressed to determine the earliest history of the use of mind-altering drugs by human beings. It was probably while experimenting with plants to locate sources of food that the first substances with the power to alter the brain were discovered. Once discovered, certain individuals most likely repeated their use of the substance in an effort to achieve the same effect. The first instances of *compulsive* drug use may have developed in this manner.

Although we cannot be positive when the first use of mind-altering substances took place, we do know that the people living on the island of Cyprus in the Eastern Mediterranean Sea dissolved opium in both wine and water and exported it to Egypt as early as 1500 B.C. Centuries later, one of the most well-known recorded histories of substance-related abuse is that which caused the Opium War between China and Great Britain (1840–1842). Great Britain had brought opium into China where it was traded for other goods. This resulted in widespread addiction among the

GLOSSARY

compulsive: Behavior that is intense and often repeated.

THE BOWL.

During the nineteenth century, the medical community began to realize more fully the dangers of alcohol.

Chinese people. During the war, China unsuccessfully tried to stop the importation of opium into the country.

Also during the nineteenth century, active ingredients were extracted from opium and prescribed by physicians in the treatment of a wide variety of illnesses. Substances like morphine and cocaine were legal and readily available. Many soldiers returned home from the Civil War addicted to morphine, which had been given to them for pain caused by wounds on the battlefield. In 1874, when heroin was first produced, it was thought that this drug would provide a cure for morphine addiction. As substance-related disorders became prevalent and some individuals died because of them, people began to recognize the dangers of addiction. In the latter part of the nineteenth century and early twentieth century, countries began to pass laws to control mind-altering substances. In the early twentieth century, the United States Supreme Court ruled that physicians could no longer prescribe narcotics as part of a maintenance program for addicted individuals.

With dedication and perseverance, people can usually recover from substance-related disorders, but withdrawal symptoms are often extremely unpleasant. Until relatively recently, individuals with a substance-related disorder were expected to conquer it "cold turkey," that is, by simply discontinuing use of the substance. But discontinuing use of addictive substances is no simple matter. Treatment facilities were developed where individuals with substance-induced disorders could be safely monitored and kept away from the substance for an extended period of time. While peer-group and individual counseling sessions were often available, use of psychiatric medications was generally avoided.

This is still the way to recovery for many individuals, but over the years scientists have worked to develop psychiatric medications that can help to alleviate the symptoms of withdrawal. Medications have also been developed to help individuals avoid ***chronic*** relapse and maintain remission from some addictive substances. Professionals working today to assist in the elimination of substance-related disorders have begun to understand and appreciate the benefits of these psychiatric medications.

GLOSSARY

chronic: *Something that continues or keeps repeating.*

When she tried to conquer her dependence on heroin on her own, Tanya experienced severe withdrawal symptoms including cramps, nausea, vomiting, diarrhea, uncontrollable shaking, an accelerated heart rate, anxiety, insomnia, and panic. When she couldn't stand it any longer, she telephoned a friend, who rushed over with more heroin, and Tanya gratefully injected it into her body. After that experience, Tanya was reluctant to try to quit again. Eventually, however, she got help from a physician. He was able to alleviate her symptoms with psychiatric medication, thus making her more comfortable while she went through the withdrawal process.

The treatment facility that Tom attended relied on behavioral therapy, but psychiatric medications were admin-

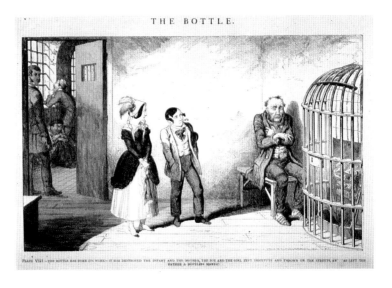

THE BOTTLE.

In the nineteenth century, people who suffered from severe addictions to alcohol were sometimes put in institutions where they could not harm themselves, but little treatment was provided. Today's treatment facilities are far more effective.

Nicotine addiction is one of the most common substance-related disorders in our society today.

istered to individuals with a demonstrated need. Tom only needed medication while going through withdrawal, and he left the facility free of all substance use, including psychiatric medications. His friend Bob, however, needed the extra assurance a prescribed medication called Antabuse provided to assist with his remission.

Early in Christiane's attempt to eliminate her use of cigarettes, she used nicotine patches. Even with the patches, however, she became depressed and found it difficult to concentrate in her classes. Successfully completing homework assignments became impossible. Christiane's doctor prescribed Zyban, an antidepressant that helped to eliminate her discomfort, thus aiding in Christiane's recovery from nicotine addiction.

Thanks to years of scientific research, these and other psychiatric medications are now available for use in the treatment of substance-related disorders.

GLOSSARY

dopamine: A chemical that is necessary for the central nervous system to function properly.

- Amantadine (Symmetrel): This medication increases *dopamine* activity in the brain. It has been used to treat symptoms of cocaine withdrawal and, sometimes, to help maintain remission.
- Benzodiazepines: Some of these sedatives, like Librium, are used to treat withdrawal from addictive sedatives such as alcohol.
- Buprenorphine (Subutex and Suboxone): Subutex can be used at the beginning of treatment for addiction to opiates, and Suboxone (which contains both buprenorphine and naloxone) can be used in maintenance treatment for addiction to opiates. This medication has not been tested in individuals under the age of sixteen.
- Bupropion (Wellbutrin and Zyban): Antidepressants that may be used during both withdrawal and remission. Safe levels have not been established for individuals under the age of eighteen. However, it is commonly prescribed for this age group. Lithium, Zoloft, Prozac and similar antidepressants have also been used in the treatment of alcohol addiction.
- Clonidine: This nonopiate is used to treat individuals with an addiction to heroin. Safety and effectiveness have not been established for individuals under the age of twelve.
- Disulfiram: (Antabuse, Sulfiram): This medication is commonly used to prevent relapse of alcohol abuse and less frequently to discourage use of cocaine.
- Methadone: Probably the most well-known opiate used to treat addiction to heroin. Levo-alpha-acetylmethadol is a longer acting form of methadone.
- Naltrexone (ReVia) and Naloxone (Narcan): These opiate-blocking drugs are sometimes used to treat individuals suffering from an overdose. Naltrexone is also used to help individuals avoid relapse by reduc-

ing cravings for cocaine, alcohol, and sometimes heroin. Safe use for individuals under the age of eighteen has not been established for naltrexone. Clinical experience regarding use of naloxone in individuals under the age of twelve is limited.

Phencyclidine, sleep aids, and amphetamines have a serious potential for abuse.

DISULFIRAM

GLOSSARY

metabolize: Break down for use by the natural physical and chemical processes occurring in the body.

Most medications are studied for many years before they are approved for use. But the history of disulfiram is interesting as its therapeutic qualities were discovered quite by accident in the 1930s. The substance was used in the rubber industry, where a group of workers was exposed to it. When the workers later drank alcohol, they became ill. Thus scientists began to realize that this nontoxic substance interferes with the ability of the body to *metabolize* alcohol. In science, new information builds upon prior knowledge. Once scientists realized the connection between tetraethylthiuram and the use of alcohol, studies could be conducted and medication could be developed and approved for use.

Heroin is an addictive chemical.

Brand Names vs. Generic Names

Talking about psychiatric drugs can be confusing, because every drug has at least two names: its "generic name" and the "brand name" that the pharmaceutical company uses to market the drug. Generic names come from the drugs' chemical structures, while brand names are used by drug companies in order to inspire public recognition and loyalty for their products.

Here are the brand names and generic names for some common psychiatric drugs used to treat substance disorders:

Antabuse®	disulfiram
Ativan®	lorazepam
Halcion®	triazolam
Klonopin®	clonazepam
Librium®	chlordiazepoxide
Prozac®	fluoxetine hydrochloride
ReVia®	naltrexone
Serax®	oxazepam
Symmetrel®	amantadine
Valium®	diazepam
Wellbutrin®	bupropion
Zoloft®	sertraline hydrochloride

BENZODIAZEPINES

Discovered in the 1950s with the introduction of Librium, benzodiazepines have been available since the 1960s. But the story of their origin is really much older than that. Research that led to their development was based on the dis-

BEAVERTON HIGH LIBRARY

Antidepressants can be helpful when a person is trying to quit smoking.

GLOSSARY

synthesize: To form a new substance from parts of others.

tranquilizing: Having a calming, quieting influence.

covery in 1864 of barbituric acid by Adolph von Baeyer, a German chemist. Research involving barbiturates led to the development of benzodiazepines, which now includes a dozen drugs such as Valium, Halcion, and Triazolam, along with Librium, Serax, Klonopin, Restoril, and Xanax. But the first of these antianxiety medications to be discovered was Librium, and it was discovered quite by accident in 1955 at the Hoffman-LaRoche pharmaceutical company. A chemist named Leo Sternbach was the first to **synthesize** Librium, but initially he did not realize how the chemical could be used or what the effects of use would be. In fact, the substance was set aside while other projects were worked on, and it was essentially forgotten for two years. At that point, the forgotten chemical was rediscovered while cleaning the facilities, and new testing was begun. The drug's **tranquilizing** quality was discovered when it was tested on animals in the laboratory. It was also noted that the chemical caused muscle relaxation. After considerable more testing, the chemical, called chlordiazepoxide, was made available as Librium.

While researchers were studying Librium, more benzo-diazepines were synthesized. Some of these substances are more addictive than others, however. Diazepam (Valium) was the second benzodiazepine to go on the market, and it is considerably more potent than Librium. It is the less ad-dictive forms, like Librium, that are generally used in the treatment of substance-related disorders. For over thirty years Librium has been used to blunt withdrawal symptoms associated with alcohol addiction and to reduce the chance that a person might have a seizure during withdrawal.

BUPROPION

Before medications can be legally sold in North America, they undergo years of testing conducted in clinical trials. These trials are conducted by companies, individuals, and universities across North America. During these tests, a medication is administered to specific groups of people un-der very controlled circumstances with the results being carefully collected and studied. Then hearings are held where testimony is taken prior to a decision being made on whether or not to approve use of the pharmaceutical.

During the 1970s, clinical trials were conducted to de-termine the effectiveness of bupropion as an antidepres-sant. Hearings held in the 1980s recommended it for approval. Just as the medication was about to reach the market, however, another study showed that a group of sub-jects with ***bulimia*** had an increase in seizures as a result of

> **GLOSSARY**
>
> ***bulimia:*** *An eating disorder charac-terized by periods of binge eating followed by purg-ing episodes (through self-induced vomiting or the use of laxa-tives) or other methods to con-trol weight.*

bupropion use. This finding delayed introduction of bupropion to the market. Eventually the medication did become available with an established maximum dosage level. Antidepressants like bupropion are sometimes now used to assist in the cessation of smoking.

BUPRENORPHINE

The National Institute on Drug Abuse has funded many of these scientific studies, including some on buprenorphine and buprenorphine used in combination with naloxone for the treatment of opiate addiction. These studies were con-

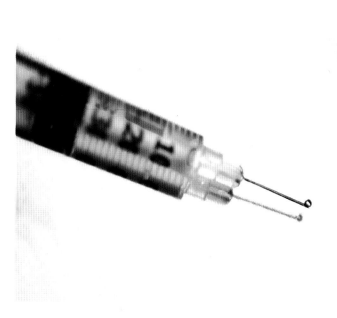

Methadone was first used as a painkiller. Today it frequently plays a role in treating heroin addiction.

Drug Approval

Before a drug can be marketed in the United States, it must be officially approved by the Food and Drug Administration (FDA). Today's FDA is the primary consumer protection agency in the United States. Operating under the authority given it by the government, and guided by laws established throughout the twentieth century, the FDA has established a rigorous drug approval process that verifies the safety, effectiveness, and accuracy of labeling for any drug marketed in the United States.

While the United States has the FDA for the approval and regulation of drugs and medical devices, Canada has a similar organization called the Therapeutic Product Directorate (TPD). The TPD is a division of Health Canada, the Canadian government department of health. The TPD regulates drugs, medical devices, disinfectants, and sanitizers with disinfectant claims. Some of the things that the TPD monitors are quality, effectiveness, and safety. Just as the FDA must approve new drugs in the United States, the TPD must approve new drugs in Canada before those drugs can enter the market.

ducted in cooperation with a private company that manufactures medications, Reckitt & Colman Pharmaceuticals, Inc. The goal of the five-year studies was to collect the data necessary to obtain new drug approval for buprenorphine and make it available in North America. The studies concluded that buprenorphine is more effective than methadone when prescribed in low doses and that consistent intake of buprenorphine resulted in a reduction of opiate use.

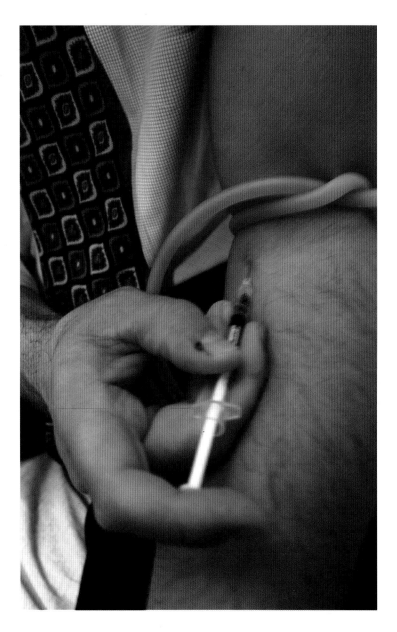

Not all heroin addicts are street junkies. Some are business-people and professionals.

METHADONE

First developed in Germany where it was used as an **analgesic**, methadone (a synthetic opiate) came into use in North America after World War II. Although it is different from morphine chemically, its effects on the brain are very similar. In the 1950s methadone began to be used for the control of withdrawal symptoms during detoxification from opiates. Doctors Vincent Dole and Marie Nyswander are credited with the promotion of this substance during the latter 1960s for use in the rehabilitation of individuals addicted to narcotics.

In 1964, Dole and Nyswander conducted a year-long study of methadone at Rockefeller University. Six men who were addicted to heroin volunteered to live in a hospital in New York City, where they were kept in a controlled environment and given a specific diet for the duration of the study. Except for the fact that they were addicted to heroin, all of the men were in good physical health. First, the subjects were given controlled amounts of morphine by injection eight times per day. During that time Dr. Dole and Dr. Nyswander monitored their physiological, **metabolic**, and **biochemical** states. The researchers were trying to discover if physiological factors cause addiction and relapse into addiction after remission.

The study determined that tolerance to morphine grew quickly, after which the men became more anxious and requested larger doses of the drug. This reaction demonstrated the failure of morphine as a treatment for addiction to narcotics. The researchers then substituted oral doses of methadone for the morphine and studied the results. When the subjects were placed on methadone, unexpected behavioral changes began to take place. For example, while using morphine, the subjects had remained unproductive and, except for demanding larger doses of morphine, showed little

GLOSSARY

analgesic: *A substance that eliminates or lessens the feeling of pain.*

metabolic: *Caused by the chemical processes in the body.*

biochemical: *The chemical processes in a living being.*

A person who is addicted to heroin . . .

interest in anything. After the switch to methadone maintenance, however, the subjects no longer craved heroin. In
fact, they became more relaxed and better adjusted. The
men began functioning normally. After the study, one of the
men, who had previously dropped out of high school and
even spent some time in prison, completed school and went
on to earn a degree in aeronautical engineering.

Nyswander and Dole decided to conduct additional
studies with more individuals who were addicted to heroin.
In 1965, they published their findings in the *Journal of the
American Medical Association.* The subjects involved in subsequent studies lived in unlocked hospital wards where they
were immediately placed on methadone. After the proper
maintenance level was established, they could leave the hospital periodically with supervision. Later in the study, they
were allowed to go home but had to return to the hospital

. . . needs to shoot up more and more often in order to satisfy his uncontrollable craving for the drug.

Unfortunately, there are more people addicted to heroin than there are methadone clinics to treat them.

daily to receive their methadone medication. The medication was consumed under observation by a nurse in order to be certain that the substance was not saved and then later sold. A urine sample was required and tested to be certain the people in the study had not relapsed into heroin use.

The final goal of the study was to integrate the individuals back into the social structure of society. All of the subjects in these studies had previously attempted to discontinue heroin use but had failed. With methadone maintenance the subjects reported that their previously uncontrollable craving for heroin had ceased. Moreover, when heroin was administered to members of the study, it did not have the same effects as it did when used prior to the study. The conclusion of the researchers was that methadone was acting to block the effects of heroin, thus preventing the subjects from having a "high" experience during heroin use. In other words, by preventing an individual from gaining the desired effect of heroin, methadone was discouraging the use of the narcotic. Additionally, the researchers noted that the individuals performed within normal ranges on all psychological and medical tests. The individuals on methadone maintenance were basically indistinguishable from individuals without a substance-induced disorder.

This ground-breaking study formed the basis for the methadone-maintenance program in North America. By 1973, the number of individuals enrolled in the program had already grown to approximately 40,000. Today it is estimated that one fourth of the people addicted to heroin in the United States have received methadone treatment; however, there are not enough methadone clinics to treat all of the individuals who are in need.

GLOSSARY

placebo: A material without drug activity but whose appearance is identical to an active drug; it is used in clinical trials of new medications.

NALTREXONE

In 1986, the University of Pennsylvania/VA Center for Studies of Addiction conducted the first human clinical trial of naltrexone as a treatment for alcoholism. Half of the individuals participating in the study were given naltrexone as part of their maintenance program, and the other half were given a ***placebo***. The group taking naltrexone reported a significant decrease in their craving for alcohol and had a decreased incidence of relapse compared to the group that was given the placebo. It must be noted, however, that use of naltrexone did not prevent individuals from ingesting a small amount of alcohol, since about half of those in each group did report having one or two drinks. The data showed that when an individual taking naltrexone gave in to the craving to use alcohol, he was much less likely to fall back into a pattern of abuse. The Food and Drug Administration approved the use of naltrexone for treatment of alcoholism in 1994.

NICOTINE

Nicotine, the addictive substance in cigarettes, is sometimes used in the form of gum and patches to help individuals quit smoking. In the 1970s, a Swedish company began to study a chewing gum that would deliver nicotine to the body. More than ten years were spent in studying the substance before the Food and Drug Administration approved it for use in the United States in 1984. Canada had approved the gum several years before. The gum has undergone several studies in which it was proven that it does decrease the desire to smoke among those addicted to cigarettes.

You may be wondering why it is better to have nicotine enter your body by chewing gum or wearing a patch than to obtain it by smoking. It is simply safer to have it enter the body through the skin than to inhale it (and the other hazardous substances found in cigarettes) into your lungs. But nicotine is definitely not good for you in any form. The goal is to use the gum or patches to stop the craving for cigarettes and then to decrease the amount used until the gum or patches are no longer necessary.

Some of the medications listed in this chapter were initially developed to treat other conditions, and then later researchers discovered that these chemicals could also be used to help individuals with substance-related disorders. Amantadine, for example, is usually used to treat individuals with influenza and also for the treatment of Parkinson's disease. Buprenorphine is a painkiller.

Though none of the psychiatric medications we have discussed provides a cure for substance-related disorders, some of them assist individuals in recovering from addiction by lessening withdrawal symptoms. Others can help users maintain their remission from substance dependence once it is achieved. The history of the psychiatric drugs used to treat substance-related disorders is long, and research to discover new medications and treatments continues.

Drug treatment for substance-related disorders is designed to help people cope with withdrawal symptoms while freeing them from their addictions.

3 | How Do the Drugs Work?

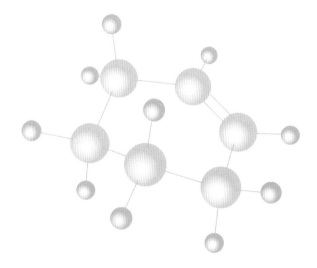

Drug therapies are tailored to individuals based on the person's psychological and physical needs and on the specific substance(s) causing the disorder. Medications that are administered during withdrawal are provided in an effort to minimize withdrawal symptoms. This is usually accomplished by using medications that produce effects similar to the substance that is the cause of the disorder. In other words, if someone is addicted to a sedative, a different sedative might be used to lessen the symptoms of withdrawal. To better understand why this works, let's take a look at the brain.

A brain is like a complicated machine. It's filled with cells and chemicals that are engaged in countless and constant interactions. Your brain runs your entire body. It makes sure that you keep breathing and that your heart keeps pumping. It tells you to eat when you are hungry and to go to sleep when you're tired. Your brain decides whom you like and whom to avoid, when to watch television and

GLOSSARY

compound: A combination of two or more separate elements.

when to read a book, if you want to play baseball or if you'd rather go out for track.

The brain and the body are in constant communication through neurotransmitters. A neurotransmitter is a chemical *compound* that is released from the end of a nerve in the brain. From there it passes across a gap, called a synapse, and then activates the receiving end (called the dendrite) of another nerve. The receiving nerve then transmits a neurotransmitter to the next nerve, and this process is repeated. Receptors are small areas on each dendrite. These receptors are sensitive to the neurotransmitter that has been released by the sending nerve.

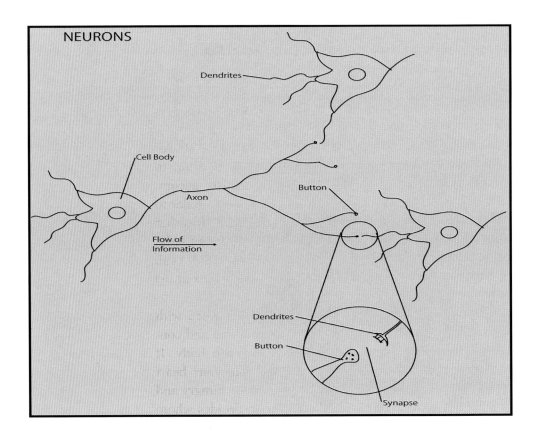

NEURONS

Dendrites

Cell Body

Axon

Button

Flow of Information

Dendrites

Button

Synapse

Addictive substances cause powerful actions in the human brain by interacting and interfering with the mechanisms your brain uses to send information from one cell to another. Imagine that your brain is like a computer that's running all the assembly lines in a factory. If you poured a glass of water onto the computer, you would short-circuit the assemblage of wires, transmitters, and connections. In a way, addictive substances short-circuit your brain.

The psychiatric drugs that are used during treatment of substance-related disorders also cause powerful actions in the brain. However, they are administered carefully by physicians in an effort to counteract some of the symptoms that can occur during withdrawal from an addictive substance or to increase the likelihood that the individual will be able to resist using the addictive substance in the future.

To guarantee the greatest chance for success, drug therapy should be part of a larger treatment program that includes counseling. Some individuals with substance-related disorders are able to recover with counseling alone, but others are unable to begin serious treatment without the use of psychiatric medications.

People who abuse addictive substances usually cannot gradually cut down on use. A person might try to use only a small amount of the substance to keep withdrawal symptoms under control, but then cravings for the substance become impossible to ignore. Often the individual ends up using more of the substance rather than less of it. Sometimes an individual will try to stop using these addictive substances "cold turkey," but withdrawal symptoms usually begin very quickly. As in Tanya's case mentioned in the last chapter, these symptoms can be very serious.

If an individual decides she cannot bear the withdrawal symptoms as Tanya did and chooses instead to stop the symptoms by using the substance that caused the problem

in the first place, or if she successfully gets through withdrawal only to begin using the substance again at a later date, subsequent withdrawal symptoms can be even more severe than during the first withdrawal. After that, an individual might avoid treatment because she is afraid of the severity of the withdrawal she will have to endure. For all of

When you put addictive substances into your brain, it's like pouring water into your computer—you cause a "short circuit"!

these reasons it is best to conquer a substance-related disorder with medical supervision from an individual who can prescribe necessary medications, recommend or conduct psychological therapies, and exert total control over use of any addictive substances.

As stated previously, some psychiatric medications used to help an individual **detoxify** produce effects that are similar to the addictive substance. In this way they help to minimize withdrawal symptoms. Other psychiatric medications interfere with an abusive substance's ability to activate certain areas of the brain.

To simplify this idea, imagine that there is a football game going on in your head. The quarterback is like a nerve ending in the brain. He throws the ball (which is like a neurotransmitter), which then passes over a portion of the football field (the synapse) to the receiving end (called the dendrite) of another football player (another nerve). Think of the fingers of the receiving football player as receptors on the end of his hands (which are like the dendrites in the brain). The receiver's fingers (receptors) are sensitive to the football (neurotransmitter) that has been released by the quarterback (sending nerve). In your brain football game, there are many quarterbacks throwing many balls to their receivers. When you introduce addictive substances into your body, you disrupt all the rules of the brain football game. Imagine that suddenly extra balls are all over the place, being shot at various receivers. Psychiatric medications are like new players who have been introduced to help control the chaos. They may throw a ball at a receiver so that when the receiver catches it, his hands will be full and he will not be able to catch a more harmful ball. Other psychiatric medications are like blockers that keep the bad "footballs" from reaching the intended receivers.

GLOSSARY

detoxify: To remove a poison.

DRUGS THAT TREAT COCAINE ADDICTION

Consider Greg's experience with cocaine, which acts as a stimulant in the body. When Greg used cocaine it stimulated his central nervous system, which then caused a feeling of excitement, a heightening of his senses, an accelerated heart rate, and a reduced desire for sleep. Greg also felt more self-confident, and he had a greater sense of well-being. He wanted to continue having these feelings, but cocaine is a short-acting drug, which means that the desired effects don't last very long. Individuals who inhale cocaine often want to use the substance again after only ten to thirty minutes. Even at the beginning, Greg came down from it quickly. That made him depressed, and he immediately began to think about how he could get more cocaine so that he could experience the exciting feelings again. Before long, Greg's *tolerance* grew, and the amount of cocaine that he initially used was no longer enough to produce the effect he craved. As a result, Greg began to use ever-increasing doses of the drug. When he first experimented with cocaine, Greg was snorting it, but he progressed quickly to using it in all forms, including injections. By the time Greg sought treatment, he was a compulsive user. It seemed like no matter how many hits of cocaine Greg took, it was never enough.

At Greg's level of use, new and frightening symptoms sometimes occurred; for example, he heard unpleasant voices that terrified him. Other times he felt like bugs were crawling on his body. When this happened, his heart would pound so fast he was afraid he was going to have a heart attack. These symptoms are typical of individuals who, like Greg, have been using cocaine in high doses over an extended

> It is estimated that more than 640,000 people in North America use cocaine at least once per week.

GLOSSARY

tolerance: *The ability of the body to withstand exposure to something.*

period of time. Eventually Greg experienced a seizure, which led to hospitalization and his decision to do everything possible to end his addiction.

Greg knew what to expect, because he had already experienced withdrawal symptoms many times when he was

Greg was fortunate to have sought treatment when he did; heart attacks and strokes are two of the dangers of long-term use of cocaine.

between doses of cocaine. Symptoms of withdrawal from stimulants are not as obviously dramatic as withdrawal from sedatives, and they usually subside gradually over one to three weeks. An increased need for sleep is one of the major symptoms of stimulant withdrawal. Unfortunately, it is combined with anxiety and depression, and these feelings can be longer lasting. If feelings like this do persist, antidepressant medication may be indicated.

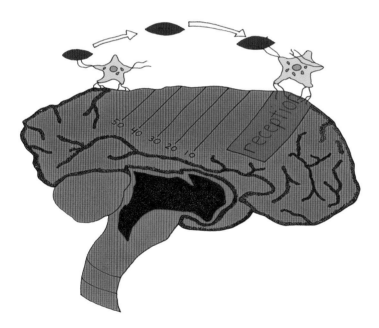

The messages being passed between nerve cells is a little like a football game going on inside your brain.

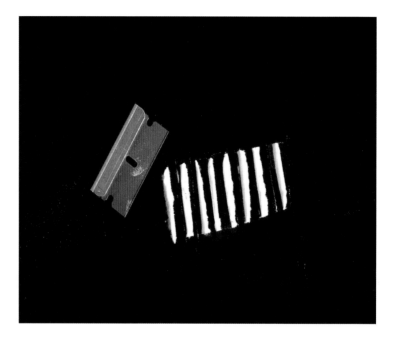

People addicted to cocaine crave the drug because of the heightened feelings of pleasure it gives them.

One of the major challenges in helping someone overcome an addiction to cocaine is encouraging him to resist the lingering urge to use the substance. Greg was physically and emotionally dependent on cocaine, and despite the negative experiences he sometimes had when using it, he experienced a continuous and extreme craving for the substance. One cause of this craving was the fact that cocaine increases dopamine activity in the brain. Along with dopamine, cocaine also keeps both noradrenaline and serotonin active in the brain. These chemicals are responsible for heightened experiences of pleasure.

Remember that when you become addicted to a substance, you interfere with the brain's natural chemical activities. As the brain becomes accustomed to the addictive substances that are being introduced to it on a more and more regular basis, it begins to compensate for their presence. This is when tolerance builds, which causes the need to use ever-increasing amounts of the substance in order to achieve the desired effect. Trying to eliminate the substance after the brain has built up a tolerance to it causes yet more chemical disruption in the brain. Greg interfered with the natural chemical activity in his brain when he began using cocaine, and later, when he tried to discontinue use of cocaine, he altered his brain chemistry yet again. That's when withdrawal symptoms began to occur in his body.

The psychiatric medication called amantadine also increases dopamine activity in the brain by releasing dopamine from its storage sites. Taking amantadine can, therefore, reduce symptoms of cocaine withdrawal. Antidepressants are also sometimes administered to individuals during withdrawal from cocaine and immediately thereafter, since many people who have become addicted to cocaine experience depression during these times. Greg was aided through his withdrawal by both of these medications. There is no scientific proof that treatment with antidepressants helps to curb relapse; when Greg's treatment with amantadine ended, he may have relied just as much on his strong determination and the assistance he received from counseling to avoid falling into a relapse.

DRUGS THAT TREAT ALCOHOLISM

Alcohol is dangerous because of the potential for dependence and also because, taken at high and continuous lev-

GLOSSARY

delirium tremens:
A change in con-
sciousness, think-
ing ability, or at-
tention caused by
alcohol with-
drawal.

els, it can cause brain damage as well as liver damage. The risks of cancer and heart disease are also elevated for heavy users of alcohol. Many people have recovered from dependence on alcohol through counseling programs at residential facilities that do not use medical supplements. Other individuals have been helped tremendously by psychiatric medications as part of their treatment programs.

Benzodiazepines

Benzodiazepines, especially Librium, Ativan, and Serax, have been used by many doctors to block serious withdrawal symptoms (such as **delirium tremens**) caused when a person with an addiction to alcohol discontinues use of that substance. Any of the benzodiazepines could be used for this, but the potential for abuse of some of these substances is lower than it is for others, because some are less addictive than others. Serax may be the best choice for individuals who have suffered liver damage as a result of alcohol addiction because this drug is not metabolized by the liver.

Alcohol can cause brain damage both in the user and, for women who are pregnant, in the fetus. The most common cause of mental retardation is fetal alcohol syndrome.

Sedatives (like alcohol) work by reducing activity in the brain to a level that makes a person feel calmer, less anxious, more relaxed. Sometimes individuals have become dependent on alcohol as a result of untreated anxiety problems. Trying to self-medicate, that is to regulate your mood with chemical substances, can lead to substance addiction. If a psychiatric evaluation or subsequent therapy reveals that a person with a substance-related disorder suffers from anxiety or depression, an antidepressant may be prescribed during treatment. The physician is treating the person's anxiety or depression so that she will be less tempted to turn to the addictive substance. The doctor is not treating the addiction itself.

If a person drinks alcohol while taking Antabuse, she will become extremely sick.

Antabuse

Antabuse works in maintenance programs for alcohol addiction because the individual desires to avoid the negative consequences of using alcohol while taking this substance. An individual using this treatment option would begin taking Antabuse after completing withdrawal from alcohol. Unfortunately, Antabuse does not reduce a person's craving for alcohol. It does, however, interfere with the body's ability to metabolize alcohol. If a person gives in to his craving and begins to consume alcohol while taking Antabuse, a toxic substance called acetylaldehyde will begin to build up in his body. This produces uncomfortable symptoms, including nausea and vomiting. The individ-

ual's skin turns a purplish color. In severe cases, even more serious effects, including respiratory distress and heart attacks, can occur. Antabuse is also sometimes effective in treating cocaine addiction, perhaps because it increases certain negative symptoms, such as edginess and paranoia, associated with cocaine use. Antabuse can be a powerful motivator for alcohol avoidance, but it has several risks. For instance, small quantities of alcohol like that found in some foods, sometimes even inhaled traces of alcohol, can induce these negative consequences.

DRUGS THAT TREAT OPIATE ADDICTION

In some ways, addiction to opiates, such as heroin, is the opposite of addiction to cocaine or amphetamines. Whereas those chemicals produce feelings of excitement, opiates act as a depressant on the central nervous system, making the individual feel relaxed and calm. Pain is reduced and sleep often results. It should be noted that nausea and respiratory depression, even death, can also result from the use of opiates. Opiates act in the brain by interfering with the body's natural painkillers: endorphins and enkephalins.

As with other addictive substances, when people use opiates, their brains try to compensate, in this case by producing chemicals to counteract the effects of elevated opiate levels. As the addictive substance is taken over and over again, the brain becomes accustomed to these new chemical levels and begins to react automatically. Soon the brain is compensating for extra opiate levels whether or not the individual actually uses the substance. When the brain acts in this habitual way, a physical dependence on the opiates has occurred and more of the opiate is needed for the individual to achieve the desired effect. At this point, the indi-

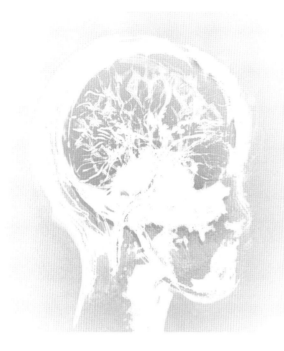

Opiates have a powerful chemical effect on the brain.

vidual can experience withdrawal symptoms even though she may not have any intention of cutting back on use of the opiate. She may just not have immediate access to another dose of the substance. A very dangerous pattern has begun, which sets the individual on a path of continued and escalating opiate use. Tanya's story is typical of this scenario.

As far back as she could remember, everyone in Tanya's family had praised her intelligence. "What a crackerjack that little Tanya is!" Tanya remembered the way her grandfather's big, booming voice echoed through the sparsely fur-

nished home he shared with her family. If he could see her now, she guessed he wouldn't think she was so smart. *Granddad must be rolling over in his grave. Don't look at me Gramps. I'm so sorry, but I don't have a choice anymore.*

New thoughts piled up on old ones as Tanya stuck the needle in her arm. She liked the needle now—loved the needle really. Thoughts of the needle were always floating around in her head along with Grandpa. Her mother was there, too, and her little sister. *How can I continue to let everyone down? I'm worthless, but I'm so sorry.*

Mary, Tanya's mother, never gave up on her daughter, but there was little she could do to curb Tanya's use of heroin. She knew Tanya had tried to give up the substance at least once, but she wasn't able to do it. Mary's once-intelligent daughter had fallen head over heals in love with the substance that was ruining her life—ruining all of their lives.

No amount of reasoning had any effect on Tanya now, so her mother had turned to her faith for comfort. Her friends at the church she attended offered her solace in her world turned upside down. And at her church, she met Dr. Baeten, who shared with the entire church community his own story of substance dependence.

As Mary listened, she felt her first faint wisp of hope. She was certain that if Dr. Baeten could recover from his dependence on prescription drugs, save his practice, and become the respected member of the community he was today, Tanya could overcome her addiction, too. After the service, Mary shared her situation, her hopes, and her fears with this knowledgeable and sympathetic man, and she was overjoyed when he agreed to intervene in Tanya's situation.

Dr. Baeten immediately took note of Tanya's deteriorated health. He didn't need to conduct a battery of tests to see that she was severely malnourished and in real danger

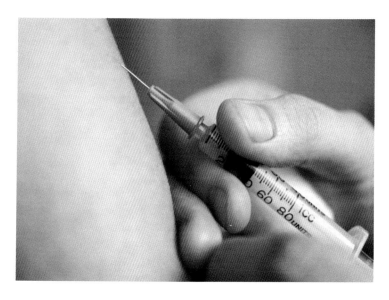

A person who uses heroin frequently will have "tracks"—scars on her skin from frequent injections.

because of it. He also couldn't help but notice the needle marks on her arms. Obviously Tanya was a heavy user. Dr. Baeten knew Tanya could overdose and suffer serious consequences, maybe even die. If she overdosed and someone got her to a hospital in time, she could be treated with naloxone to reverse the symptoms, but what if she was alone or if the people she did drugs with were as out of it as she was? It was time for Tanya to save her own life—and he was going to help her do it.

Tanya was ready. She often hated herself for using heroin, and she wanted her old self back. She wanted to be the intelligent, successful person she knew people had assumed she would turn into when she was younger. But she realized she couldn't take the first steps toward becoming that person alone.

Methadone

Because Tanya became extremely depressed during her withdrawal from heroin, her treatment involved long-term use of methadone. Methadone affects the same receptors in the brain as does heroin, thereby blocking the effect of heroin and reducing the individual's craving for it. Because methadone is a longer acting opiate than is heroin (which means it affects the body for a longer period of time—one or two days as opposed to three to six hours for heroin), re-peated doses are not needed as often. Additionally, while heroin can have a dangerous, even fatal effect on the respi-ratory system, methadone does not. The goal with Tanya, as with most individuals being treated with methadone, was to keep both cravings and withdrawal symptoms in control

There are a variety of drug treatments available for substance-related disorders.

while gradually reducing the dose of methadone needed for this purpose.

An additional benefit of methadone treatment is that it helps to reduce the excessive stress response that often plagues people addicted to heroin. Individuals on an established dose of methadone do not experience a "high" or exhibit any impairment due to the use of the medication once a tolerance level has been established. This treatment has been most successful when administered initially on an inpatient basis so the ability to obtain heroin during treatment is eliminated. Dr. Baeten also helped Tanya locate a counselor and a support group to help her deal with her relationships and other stresses in her life.

Other Drug Treatments for Opiate Addiction

Clonidine offers a medical alternative to methadone treatment because it eliminates certain withdrawal symptoms of both heroin and methadone, including nausea. It does this by damping down the brain's ***noradrenal*** system, which becomes overactive during heroin withdrawal. Essentially, it blocks the extra excitement that occurs in the central nervous system when a person who has a dependency on heroin fails to deliver the expected dose to her brain. It does not lessen the individual's anxiety or craving for heroin, however. For this reason, methadone is used more often to help people resist heroin. If necessary, clonidine can be used later to assist in withdrawal from methadone.

Naltrexone is an ***antagonist*** that can be used to remove opiates from someone's system. An affect of naltrexone, however, is to make symptoms of opiate withdrawal even worse. Naltrexone can be administered after withdrawal symptoms have ceased as an anticraving drug to help prevent an individual from returning to heroin use. However, it

GLOSSARY

noradrenal: *A substance that is both a neurotransmitter and a hormone that causes narrowing of blood vessels.*

antagonist: *A chemical that interferes with the physiology of another chemical.*

has not worked as well as methadone at helping individuals with a substance dependence on heroin.

Naltrexone works by blocking opiate receptors. Because alcohol also stimulates opiate receptors in the brain, naltrexone blocks the pleasure caused by alcohol consumption. Naltrexone can, therefore, be successfully used in maintenance programs for individuals who have developed an addiction to alcohol. In fact, research conducted at several treatment facilities has found that use of naltrexone in maintenance programs can reduce serious alcoholic relapse by as much as 50 percent.

Studies have shown that buprenorphine, like methadone, is long acting and produces opiate effects on the brain. It has been used to reduce heroin withdrawal symptoms and to help reduce the craving for heroin. An additional benefit is that if an individual injects heroin while using buprenorphine, the buprenophine will act as an opiate blocker, thus preventing the individual from having the desired heroin experience.

DRUG TREATMENT FOR MARIJUANA ADDICTION

When used in low doses, cannabis (marijuana) acts as a painkiller and sedative, affecting the brain in a manner similar to alcohol. More serious effects, including hallucinations, can occur when cannabis is used in higher doses. Some people who use cannabis experience increasingly negative effects over time. Although withdrawal symptoms are not as common as with some of the other addictive substances, insomnia, irritability, and sometimes more unpleasant symptoms can be experienced. As is the case with other substance-related disorders, these symptoms can be treated with medications.

Off-Label Prescriptions

The FDA bases its approval on specific research results. Sometimes, a particular use for a drug may have been thoroughly researched by many studies, while other uses lack the same amount of research. In that case, the drug label will only include the uses that have met the FDA's stringent research requirements. Physicians, however, may continue to prescribe that drug for other "off-label" uses.

DRUG TREATMENT FOR NICOTINE ADDICTION

Nicotine, the active ingredient in cigarettes, is one of the most unusual drugs because it has both stimulant and sedative qualities. This is probably one of the reasons why such a broad range of people fall victim to dependence on it. If a person is anxious, it can calm her down, while it can make someone who is feeling depressed feel better. In certain ways, nicotine's effect on the brain is actually quite similar to that of cocaine, but it also relaxes the individual. It is very short acting, however, and the shorter acting a substance is, the easier it is to develop a dependence on it.

Unfortunately, while a cigarette may make a person feel better emotionally, it attacks them physically. You've probably heard a hundred times about the dangers of smoking. Because it is easy to fall prey to the temptations of smoking in social situations, however, it is important to remember that heart disease, cancer, and death result from smoking cigarettes.

> Some studies estimate that each cigarette smoked reduces the smoker's life by fourteen minutes.

Nicorette chewing gum releases nicotine to the body at a rate that is correlated to the intensity of chewing. The amount of nicotine that can be obtained from one piece of gum is about the same amount as can be obtained from one cigarette. When a person chews the gum, nicotine is absorbed through the mucous membranes. Individuals report noticing the effect within a few minutes of use. Nicotine patches provide a more controlled release of nicotine to the body. The idea is to make it easier for an individual who is addicted to nicotine to quit smoking by using nicotine patches or nicotine gum to gradually reduce the amount of the chemical in the body. A nicotine pill has recently been developed.

Some adolescents believe that smoking makes them appear older or more sophisticated. In reality, each cigarette they smoke shortens their lives.

Psychiatric medications are constantly being developed and refined. Although it may seem odd, medications that act on the same brain receptors as an addictive substance that caused the disorder in the first place can sometimes be used to lessen unpleasant withdrawal symptoms. Other psychiatric medications can be used to block the effects of certain addictive substances. These drugs offer hope to those who suffer from substance abuse addiction.

A person with a drinking problem is not ready for treatment until he recognizes his condition.

4 | Treatment Descriptions

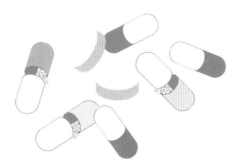

Like many individuals who develop a substance-related disorder, Tom spent a certain amount of time in denial before he finally sought treatment. At first, he told himself he drank only at parties. After he started drinking on other occasions, he told himself he was just bored, then just experimenting, and finally just relaxing. *I don't need to drink, I want to drink. I can stop any time, I just don't want to yet.* All these thoughts went through his head—right along with the alcohol that was affecting his brain.

Individuals are not ready for treatment until they recognize that they have a substance-related disorder. Often family members, friends, and medical professionals can help the individual realize that the condition exists and that he needs treatment. Once an individual does understand that he has a substance-related disorder, unless he is involved in a crisis situation (such as an overdose of the substance or severe withdrawal symptoms that warrant emergency treatment), it's a good idea to review all of the options for treatment before entering a program.

Some individuals with a substance-related disorder seek treatment either individually or with the support of family and friends. Others are forced into treatment by the courts after being arrested for possession or use of illegal substances. A person's background, motivation, and system of support are all important factors to consider when determining the ideal approach to treatment for that person.

In the past, treatment options for substance-related disorders were limited to "cold turkey"—simply discontinuing use of the substance. But as we understand now, discontinuing use of an addictive substance is no simple matter. In the last chapter we learned about many of the psychiatric drugs that are available to assist people in ridding their bodies of addictive chemicals and how these medications work. In this chapter we'll take a look at how they are administered.

With substance-related disorders, it is important to remember that a treatment option that leads to lasting remission for one person may not work for another. Treatment must be tailored to meet the needs of the individual. A good first step in the treatment of a substance-related disorder is for the individual to obtain a physical examination and a psychiatric assessment. Some psychiatric medications react with other medications, so it is important for the physician to obtain a history that includes all the medications an individual is already taking. A psychiatric assessment is necessary to determine if there are underlying causes for substance abuse, anxiety or depression for example, which also warrant treatment.

Often a combination of therapies is used in recovery from a substance-related disorder, including behavioral and vocational education, as well as psychiatric medications. Some psychiatric drug treatments can be adminis-

Physicians, psychiatrists, and advanced practice nurses are all qualified to help patients with a variety of medical and psychiatric conditions.

tered by any physician, including general practitioners, as well as psychiatrists. Other psychiatric medications, such as buprenorphine, can only be prescribed by physicians who have met specific qualifying requirements. These physicians must notify the Secretary of Health and Human Services that they are planning to prescribe this medication to treat an individual with a dependence on opioids. Behavioral therapy is administered by various professionals, including psychiatrists, social workers, and other counselors. Some treatment programs use group therapy sessions that include individuals who are recovering from substance-related disorders.

While residential facilities are prevalent, including therapeutic communities, hospitals, group homes, and halfway

Nicotine is the most deadly and addictive drug.

Drug Quiz

Which is the most deadly drug?
Which is the most addictive drug?
Which is the most widely used psychoactive drug?

The answer to the first two questions is nicotine.
The answer to the third question is caffeine.

houses, most individuals receive nonresidential treatment. Treatment is usually most intensive in the beginning, while the individual is experiencing withdrawal, and immediately thereafter. This can involve inpatient care or an intensive outpatient program. After successfully helping the individual through detoxification and the first few weeks of substance-free living, treatments can be reduced gradually. For some addictive substances, long-term care is needed to maintain remission. Some form of treatment (usually counseling) is often continued for one or two years.

One controversial detoxification method involves the use of **general anesthesia**. With this method (called ultra rapid opiod detox), opiate-blocking medications (such as naltrexone and naloxone) are administered while the patient is unconscious. The goal is to accelerate the withdrawal process so that it will be over more quickly. Unfortunately, it can also intensify withdrawal symptoms. One line of thought on the situation is that it doesn't matter if symptoms are more intense because the individual is not conscious to experience them. Other people suggest that withdrawal is not really over after this treatment. Evidence to support this lies in the fact that doctors often follow up on the procedure by prescribing sedatives and clonidine.

GLOSSARY

general anesthesia: An anesthetic that affects the entire body. Often given during surgical procedures.

Naltrexone is also used in more conventional treatment methods for alcohol and sometimes heroin use. Before beginning a treatment program that involves naltrexone, a blood test for liver problems should be conducted on the individual. This test will be repeated during treatment to be certain the liver is not being harmed by the naltrexone. The individual should not have used heroin or other opioids for at least a week prior to beginning treatment, and blood or urine tests should be performed to confirm that no traces of heroin are left in the individual's body. To discourage heroin use by blocking the effects of heroin, naltrexone can

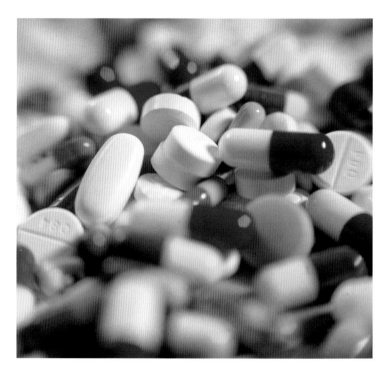

Many psychiatric medications are available in tablet or capsule form.

be taken in tablet form, beginning with 50 milligrams per day. The medication is effective beginning with the first dosage. Naltrexone is a long-acting drug, so often the dose can be altered to three times per week with larger doses (100 to 150 milligrams) being utilized. Individuals who are using the medication to reduce their desire to use alcohol usually continue to take 50 milligrams per day for at least six months. After that length of time, the desire for alcohol has diminished in most individuals. Additionally, by that time most people will have adjusted to alcohol-free living, so naltrexone can usually be safely eliminated from their maintenance program. Naltrexone can be administered in conjunction with an antidepressant, such as Prozac or Zoloft, if an individual is experiencing symptoms that warrant that type of medication. Some people have trouble taking medications in a consistent manner. For individuals like this, a physician could consider prescribing time-release naltrexone, which is implanted under the individual's skin. While some individuals report a reduction in heroin craving and relapse with use of naltrexone, it has not been as successful in treatment for heroin use as it has been in treatment for alcohol addiction.

TREATMENT FOR OPIATE ADDICTION

Many treatment programs for heroin addiction involve use of methadone as a stabilizing medication. Administered once per day, methadone remains effective for approximately 24 hours. Individuals are usually started on 20 milligrams per day and then increased to between 40 and 120 milligrams. Some individuals may need considerably higher doses, however. The patient should notice a decreased desire to use heroin after just one or two days of methadone

The Cost of Drug-Related Health Care
U.S. cost in 1998 = more than $9.9 billion

The Cost of Control of Illegal Drugs
U.S. cost in 1999 = $17.9 billion

---

use. Methadone maintenance is probably among the most controversial of psychiatric medication treatments. This is mainly due to the fact that individuals with a substance dependence on heroin may have to undergo treatment with methadone for an extended period of time, sometimes even for a lifetime. Methadone is usually given orally, which may help to break the habit of intravenous injection of heroin. Individuals participating in methadone maintenance programs should have an annual physical examination and blood tests. Most clinics that dispense methadone also offer counseling services. When combined with counseling, methadone treatment can be especially successful, but it is very demanding on the individual in treatment. At the beginning of the maintenance program, she must visit a clinic every day in order to obtain her medication. She will be instructed to take the medication in front of workers at the clinic so they can be certain she has actually swallowed the methadone. Once a week, she must submit a urine sample so that it can be tested for the presence of heroin.

As stated previously, clonidine is sometimes used in treatment programs for opiate addiction. It is often used in combination with sedatives. Since clonidine can lower blood pressure, the doctor should check the patient's blood pressure to be certain that it is not already low prior to treatment with this medication. Sometimes clonidine is administered to block withdrawal symptoms caused by heroin use, and it is usually effective after just a couple of doses. The individual's blood pressure should be recorded each day during this procedure. The dose is usually 0.1 to

0.3 milligrams administered three times each day for five days. After that, the dose is reduced, but treatments are continued for up to two weeks. At this point, physical symptoms of withdrawal should have subsided, but the individual may still have a strong desire to use heroin. Counseling on a long-term basis is often part of the treatment for a substance-related disorder that involves heroin. Methadone may also be prescribed to help the individual resist relapsing. Later in the treatment program, clonidine is sometimes used to help **wean** the individual off methadone.

Buprenorphine is another treatment option for those with a dependence on opioids. The individual's heart rate and breathing must be monitored during withdrawal treatment. It is administered, first as Subutex and then as Suboxone, as a daily tablet placed under the tongue where it is allowed to dissolve. Sixteen milligrams are usually given each day, but some patients respond with as little as twelve milligrams. Then dosage is adjusted up or down as needed to control withdrawal symptoms. Treatment should not be started within four hours of the patient's last opioid use.

> **GLOSSARY**
>
> **wean:** *To gradually withdraw from something.*

TREATMENT FOR ALCOHOL ADDICTION

The symptoms that appear during detoxification from alcohol addiction can be severe. Rapid pulse, fever, high blood pressure, hallucinations, and extreme agitation are all possible. A person experiencing severe withdrawal could even suffer seizures and heart failure. Symptoms such as these can cause death. That's why it is important for an individual to be under a doctor's care during alcohol withdrawal. A benzodiazepine like Librium can be used to successfully

G L O S S A R Y

intravenously:
Given directly into
the bloodstream
through a vein.

intramuscularly:
Given by an injec-
tion into a muscle.

anticonvulsant:
Something used
to prevent
seizures.

eliminate these unpleasant and dangerous symptoms of withdrawal. Prior to detoxification, the physician will have performed blood tests to determine the condition of the individual's liver. Other tests will also have been performed as part of a routine physical examination. The person's diet will be supplemented with vitamins and minerals, since alcohol depletes these necessary substances from the body. During the detoxification process, the individual's temperature will be taken frequently, and his pulse and blood pressure will be monitored closely. The hospitalized patient may be given 50 to 100 milligrams of Librium *intravenously* or *intramuscularly* and then switched to the same dose given orally every three hours. The maximum daily dose is usually 300 milligrams. The effect of the medication is felt immediately, making the individual feel calmer and somewhat sedated. Treatment is gradually reduced over the next two days, with the individual receiving smaller doses of the medication while the time between doses is extended. The medication is usually discontinued after three days. Sometimes, even though Librium has been administered to stop serious withdrawal symptoms, seizures do occur. When this happens, *anticonvulsant* medication will be administered to stabilize the patient's condition.

Since depression can be the cause of some substance-induced disorders (such as that caused by an addiction to alcohol), antidepressants can have a role in treatment. Other individuals may not have an initial history of depression but may suffer depression after detoxifying from alcohol. If psychiatric drugs, including antidepressants, are going be effective treatment options after withdrawal and outside of residential settings, they must be taken as directed. Physicians and pharmacists work hand-in-hand to explain dosages that must be taken each day, how they should be taken, when they should be taken, and so on.

Alcohol abuse has many dangers. For example, drinking and power tools are not a good combination!

When administered outside a treatment facility, it is up to the person with the substance-related disorder (and sometimes his family) to see to it that instructions are followed.

An individual should have refrained from using alcohol in any form for at least twenty-four hours before using Antabuse as a treatment. This means she cannot have eaten foods containing alcohol or used many products, including some foods, cough medicines, and even mouthwash. Applying products that contain alcohol (such as some shaving lotions) to the skin must also be avoided. Blood tests will be performed before and during treatment with Antabuse to be certain the medication does not cause any dysfunction. The first two weeks of treatment usually involve a 500-milligram tablet being administered to the individual every morning. Some people report that the medication makes them drowsy. If this happens, the drug can be taken in the evening. After

two weeks of treatment, the dose is usually reduced to one 250-milligram tablet each day. But it doesn't take two weeks for this medication to become effective. From the very first day it is active and ready to send your digestive system, blood pressure, and heart rate into turmoil if you dare to ingest alcohol. The individual taking the medication determines the length of treatment. As long as she feels like she needs the extra encouragement it provides to avoid alcohol, she can usually continue use. Some people stay on the medication for years—but anyone who is taking Antabuse should carry a medical identification card. That way, should the patient have an adverse reaction to a product containing alcohol, any medical professionals providing treatment will understand the situation and administer proper care.

Treatment for a substance-related disorder may involve an extended period of time. Many individuals do give in to

Alcohol addiction is a serious disorder that affects many levels of North American society.

use of an addictive substance after initial withdrawal and treatment, and some individuals suffer a complete relapse. This does not mean that their situation is hopeless. Instead, it is evidence that their treatment has not been completed and must be extended.

TREATMENT FOR NICOTINE ADDICTION

A physical examination is not required before using either nicotine patches or Nicorette gum to aid in conquering an addiction to cigarettes. These products are not recommended for individuals who have unregulated heart disease or for those who are pregnant, however. Withdrawal symptoms experienced when individuals who are addicted to cigarettes stop smoking can include anxiety, impatience and irritability, weight gain, depression, anger, restlessness, and trouble concentrating. Restoring nicotine to the body through the use of patches or gum can block these symptoms.

Nicotine patches are available in several brands and in various strengths. The number of cigarettes an individual usually smokes per day determines the dosage. Similarly, if using nicotine gum to aid in cessation of smoking, the number of pieces chewed per day is dependent on the usual number of cigarettes smoked in a twenty-four hour period. Each piece of gum should be chewed slowly for between twenty and thirty minutes, and the number of pieces chewed in a twenty-four hour period should never exceed thirty. Both the patch and the gum immediately begin to deliver nicotine to the body. The majority of available brands of nicotine patches are worn twenty-four hours per day, but one brand is worn for sixteen hours. An individual's craving for cigarettes should begin to diminish with the first application of a patch. As it continues to diminish, patches with reduced nicotine dosage levels should be used. The same

The earlier you start smoking, the more difficult it may be for you to stop.

Treatment can take place both in and out of residential facilities. The American Society for Addiction Medicine has devised Patient Placement Criteria that many insurance companies use to determine whether or not inpatient care is necessary. Many major universities, such as Rutgers, Columbia, New York University, and the University of Pennsylvania, sponsor research programs that deal with substance-related disorders. If the individual who desires treatment lives near one of these facilities, she or her family may want to check out the possibility of treatment there.

thing is true of the gum. A person should use fewer pieces per day as his cravings for cigarettes diminish. It usually takes several months to complete treatment and discontinue use of either the patches or the gum.

People who start smoking before the age of twenty-one, like Christiane whom we met in the first chapter, usually have the most difficult time conquering the addiction. Some individuals have been treated for this substance-related disorder with the use of bupropion rather than a nicotine product. The bupropion was administered in the form of pills and was taken for seven to twelve weeks.

Because depression is often linked to smoking, antidepressants, such as Prozac, are sometimes part of an individual's treatment. Naltrexone and clonidine have also been utilized in treatment, but thus far, nicotine itself, in the form of patches and gum, remains the major treatment for this substance-related disorder.

TREATMENT FOR CAFFEINE ADDICTION

While caffeine may be relatively harmless compared to the other chemical substances we have been discussing, it does enhance neurological activity in many areas of the brain. Most people develop tolerance to caffeine quickly. Remember that when this happens, withdrawal symptoms can result on removal of the substance. In controlled studies, some individuals experienced withdrawal symptoms (usually evidenced by fatigue) when only one or two cups of coffee per day were removed from their usual consumption. Individuals who are used to consuming higher amounts on a daily basis may experience more severe symptoms—including headaches and nausea, sometimes even vomiting—if they discontinue use. When used in high doses, caffeine can

A person who can't get through her day without regular cups of coffee may be addicted.

cause unpleasant sensations, including insomnia, muscle twitching, nervousness, rapid heart rate, and increased urination. Additionally, existing anxiety disorders can be aggravated by the use of caffeine. It is wise, therefore, to self-regulate one's intake of caffeine. An individual should be able to discontinue use or cut back on use without the aid of a complicated treatment program involving counselors and psychiatric medications.

Many psychiatric medications have the potential to cause addiction. Treatment that includes psychiatric medication must *always* be monitored by a professional who has experience in dealing with substance-related disorders. The goal of treatment for substance-related disorders is to end the individual's dependence on the substance and to restore her ability to function appropriately in society. While it is not always possible to achieve a hundred percent abstinence from an addictive substance, a reduction in use coupled with an ability to carry out family duties and employment roles is evidence of improvement.

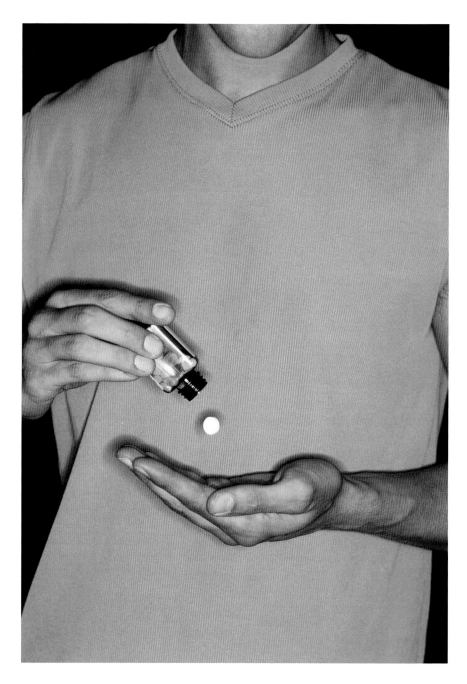

Taking painkillers for an injury can sometimes lead to addiction.

5 | Case Studies

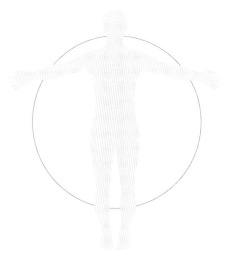

Most people are familiar with news reports of celebrities with substance-induced disorders. The deaths by drug overdose of beloved stars like Marilyn Monroe, Elvis Presley, River Phoenix, and Chris Farley touch us all. Struggles like those of Tatum O'Neal and Robert Downey Jr. break our hearts. When people like Matthew Perry seek help for a substance-related disorder, we cheer them on.

Many factors, both physical and emotional, can lead to substance-related disorders. They occur every day in the lives of thousands of individuals who aren't celebrities, like Pierre and Courtney.

PIERRE'S STORY

Ice skating was an important part of life for kids in the town where Pierre was raised. Winters in northern Quebec can be brutal, but Pierre and his brothers never noticed. Each year his father would build an ice rink in the large yard behind their home. Even though it was already dark when they re-turned from school, the boys would turn on the yard light, and if it had snowed that day, all four of them would work together to shovel the snow off the ice. They didn't want to waste any more time than necessary shoveling on the week-end when the family hockey match would begin.

Aside from school and homework, the only thing that kept Pierre off the ice was an opportunity to watch a hockey game. Of course his favorite team was the Montreal Canadi-ens, but if they weren't playing, any hockey teams would do. From as far back as he could remember, he had been watch-ing the Ottawa Senators, the Toronto Maple Leafs, the Van-couver Canucks, and he loved them all.

Pierre knew exactly what he wanted to be when he grew up. It was Pierre's dream to become a professional hockey player. So he was thrilled when his father enrolled him in the local hockey league. He enjoyed sparring on the ice with both friend and foe. He played through primary school, high school, and college, but as he grew older, hockey be-came rougher.

During college, Pierre sustained the injury that would affect much more of his future than just his career as a hockey player. During the third period of a game, one of the opposing players grabbed Pierre's right skate with his hockey stick and gave it a pull. One moment Pierre was moving forward with all the speed he could muster and the next his body was crashing down on the ice. Several mem-bers of his own team instantly joined him there as they came down on Pierre's leg, which lay stretched out behind him. A trip to the hospital emergency room determined sig-nificant injuries, and Pierre spent the remainder of the hockey season watching his teammates win the cup. Pre-scribed painkillers helped to dull the ache in his right knee

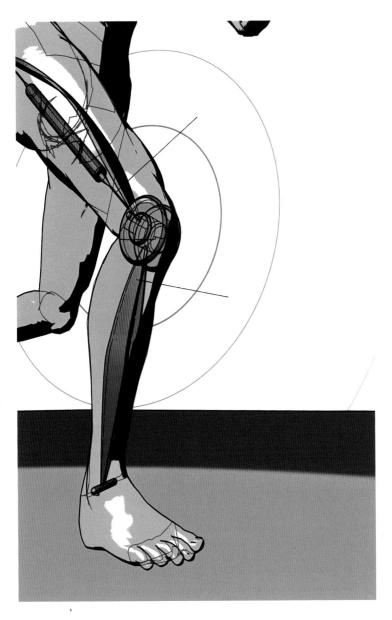

Our bodies are powerful tools—but they are also vulnerable to pain and injury.

and ankle and even made him feel a little better about not being able to participate in the final games of the season.

Strength of body and a determination to fulfill his dream despite this setback aided Pierre in his return to hockey the next season, but his leg was never quite the same. It bothered him from time to time both on and off the ice, but painkillers enabled him to continue playing the sport he loved.

Although he didn't make it to one of the big teams, Pierre did realize his dream of becoming a professional hockey player—but in these games the sport became rougher still. In his years on the ice, Pierre sustained several injuries and easily recovered from all of them, except for assaults against his right leg.

If he had been willing to give up hockey, he could have lived without the painkillers, but he couldn't continue playing without them and the team physician was willing to prescribe them. Unfortunately, Pierre also liked to stop by the

---

In his book *Recovery Options: The Complete Guide,* Joseph Volpicelli, M.D., Ph.D., lists six stages of change that define the process of recovery from use of addictive substances and points out that an individual rarely moves through them (from precontemplation to termination) in a linear manner. According to Dr. Volpicelli, people with a substance-related disorder are much more likely to move through the stages in a cyclical manner until they achieve termination.

- Precontemplation: Giving up the substance has not yet been contemplated.
- Contemplation: The individual is thinking about the situation and deciding if she wants to stop her dependence on the substance.
- Preparation: The person is getting ready to take action.
- Action: The individual is actively engaged in discontinuing substance use.
- Maintenance: Efforts are exerted to sustain remission.
- Termination: A maintenance program is no longer needed.

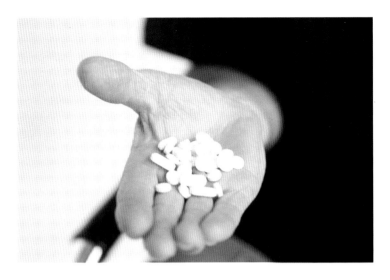

Combining painkillers with alcohol is dangerous.

pub with a couple of his teammates after each game to have a few beers. The combination of alcohol and painkillers was a dangerous one, and it led Pierre to a substance-related disorder that he failed to acknowledge for quite some time.

It also brought an end to his hockey career—and Pierre drank even more to deal with the pain of that. Pierre felt like his life was falling apart. He knew substance abuse was at the root of it, yet he couldn't stop drinking and taking pills. Eventually, with the help of his wife and his brothers, Pierre decided to seek help. He entered a treatment program where his withdrawal symptoms were managed with the careful use of antidepressant medication prescribed by the physician at the recovery center. Immediately after his withdrawal symptoms were under control, Pierre started therapy to deal with his depression. During an extended stay at the facility, he continued to take antidepressants while developing coping skills to deal with the changes in his life.

The occasional pain in his leg was managed with over-the-counter medication.

Pierre was able to conquer his addictions to both alcohol and painkillers. He returned to his family free of all substance use, and thanks to continued therapy, he was able to maintain that victory. Although he was forced to give up professional hockey, Pierre learned to appreciate and enjoy the other aspects of his life.

COURTNEY'S STORY

Sixteen-year-old Courtney liked to have fun. She was a good student, and she had never caused any serious problems for her parents. She used marijuana from time to time, which her parents would not have approved of had they known about it, but that was the extent of any substance abuse. Most of all, Courtney loved the beach. The news of her father's transfer to the Midwest came as a complete and total shock.

"You can't be serious! What do people even do there? You expect me to leave my school and all of my friends and move to some kind of cow country? I won't go. I'm calling Sarah. I'm going to ask if I can move in with her family. I guess you'll move if you want to, but I definitely don't want to, and I'm not going to."

To say that Courtney had a negative reaction to the move is an understatement. But she did move, and she hated it.

Courtney became lonely after the move, just as she had predicted. She wasn't making friends and she despised school. She hadn't even been there a week when she began waking up during the night, and she had difficulty falling back asleep. When her alarm rang, she absolutely dreaded getting up and getting dressed. Courtney's stomach felt sick

Sometimes teenagers drink in order to be socially accepted.

every day now, and anything could make her cry. She used to have a hearty appetite, but she never ate breakfast anymore. She rarely ate lunch at school because she didn't have anyone to eat with and she felt like everyone was looking at her. Walking from one class to another gave her a feeling of panic. Courtney felt as though she could hardly breathe sometimes.

Several weeks passed where nothing got better and every bad thing got worse. Courtney felt beyond miserable when her life suddenly took a turn. As Courtney entered her first class one Monday morning, she noticed a new girl sitting in the back of the room. Courtney immediately felt sorry for her. *Oh, you poor thing! I bet you just left your school and friends behind for this god-forsaken place*, she thought. The girl looked up from her desk, made eye contact with Courtney, and a smile that looked as big as California lit up her face. "Hi, I'm Melanie," she called over to Courtney. "But you can call me Mel. Everybody does."

The road to a substance-related disorder is often a long one. Many times a person does not realize where she is headed until it is too late.

"Hey Mel, I'm Courtney. Nice to meet you. Where are you from?"

"Oh, I'm not from that far away. Just about an hour west of here. How about you? I heard that you're new here too."

"Yeah, I'm from California. I've been here about a month now."

"Wow, California. You must hate it here."

"I do hate it. I haven't made a single friend. There's nothing to do here. This has to be the most boring place on the planet."

"Stick with me Courtney. I don't do boring."

For the rest of the day Courtney stuck to Melanie like glue, and she felt her life had taken an upward turn. Courtney was in awe of Melanie's ability to make friends. She made it look so easy—just tip your head down a little shyly, look up at everyone with big sad brown eyes, smile widely, say "Hi, my name is Melanie, but you can call me Mel," and that's all there seemed to be to it: Melanie had just made another friend. Why didn't it work that way for Courtney? Well, she didn't care anymore. She didn't like anyone here anyway, except for Mel that is. She'd just hang around with her.

On Thursday, Mel announced that she was going back to visit some of her old friends for the weekend and invited Courtney to join her. Courtney's parents were reluctant when she asked for permission that evening, but they had been so worried about her and so tired of watching her be sad all the time that they gave in. Mel drove her car to school on Friday and as soon as the 3:00 bell rang announcing the end of classes, the two girls were off on their adventure. But they didn't go to Mel's old friend's house as Courtney thought they would. Instead, Mel's friend was waiting for them about thirty miles outside of town. It turned out she and another girl had told their parents they'd be spending the weekend at Mel's new house. Courtney seemed to be the only one who didn't have a clue as to what was going on. That made her a little nervous, but these new girls were friendly, and she was excited to be in a group of fun-loving kids again.

"Sorry I didn't come clean with you about all the plans earlier, Court, but I didn't want you to get all nervous or anything. We're going to have some fun this weekend just like I bet you had in California. We're going to PARTY!" One of Mel's friends pulled a couple of reefers from her purse, gave one to Mel, lit up her own, and jumped back into her own car.

"Follow me ladies. I know where the fun is," she called as she turned the key and took off. Courtney hadn't smoked pot since leaving California, but she was grateful when Mel offered her the joint. Courtney took a long drag, but truth be told, she hadn't really been a party girl in California. Her ex-

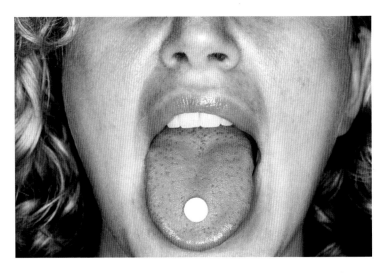

Ecstasy and other recreational pills are also dangerous chemicals with high potential for abuse.

perience with the drug scene was pretty much limited to smoking a reefer on the beach. She wasn't afraid of what lay ahead though. She was sick of nothing weekends spent away from her mean and boring non-friends at school. Anything had to be better than the life she was leading.

They needed to kill some time until dark, so they stopped at a mall. Courtney bought a few things and really enjoyed herself. After sharing a pizza and getting turned down when Mel tried to order a pitcher of beer, they hopped back in their cars and headed south. After about twenty minutes on the road, Mel pulled into the parking lot of what appeared to be a small warehouse. The lot was nearly full, and the building was pulsing with music.

"Get ready to have fun, Court. The tough times you've been having here are over. You're about to discover you don't have to be in California to have a good time."

The inside of the club was dimly lit and packed with kids who all appeared to be having the time of their lives. Courtney couldn't hear anything above the music, but she could see that Mel and her friends were regulars. They seemed to know almost everyone and they headed directly toward the back room where Ecstasy and all manner of other pills were available.

Courtney had heard about all-night parties like this one, but she had never attended one. She was nervous about the Ecstasy because she had heard that it can do permanent damage to your brain, but Mel encouraged her. "Come on, Court, you know you want to. I use them all the time, and I have one of the best brains around."

Courtney laughed nervously, and her hand trembled as she reached out for the pill. "Okay, I'm going to try one. But don't you take anything until you make sure that I'm okay."

"All right," Mel agreed, "I'll be the baby-sitter."

This began the first of many trips that Courtney would make to this place and her path to substance abuse. Ecstasy made her feel good; she couldn't believe how much energy it gave her: she really did dance all night. Later, she felt terrible, but Mel showed her which pill to take for that.

Courtney began to live for the weekends. The weeks started to get harder and harder to live through, though, so she began stocking up on more pills on Friday nights that would get her through the week: pills that brought her up when she was down, pills that relaxed her when she was nervous, pills that made her forget the world existed when she couldn't stand being in the world anymore!

It wasn't long before she couldn't get by without the pills. That scared her. She hadn't meant for her life to get like this. She decided to stop the pills and go back to California. Maybe her parents would let her go back to visit Sarah, or maybe she'd just run away.

But she couldn't stop the pills. Every time she tried she felt sick and she started having tremors. She started to think about ending the life that she had screwed up so badly.

Her parents realized that she was an emotional mess, but they had no idea about the trouble she was in until one particularly terrible night when she broke down crying and finally confided in them. They were shocked. Her mother started crying and even her father looked like he was going to lose control. Courtney had never seen them like this before, and that made her cry even harder. Her parents threw their arms around her and assured her they'd help her through this. They drove to the hospital emergency room, and she was admitted.

She had taken the first step toward recovery, but recovery wasn't easy for Courtney. She relapsed many times and went in and out of several treatment programs. Treatment with psychiatric drugs isn't right for everyone, and it wasn't right for Courtney. She had been self-medicating her anxiety and depression, but what she really needed was to develop social skills so that she could initiate conversations with people and develop friendships with them. She also needed to learn coping skills that would help her deal with difficult situations. When she entered a program that provided this type of counseling, she was finally able to recover from her substance-induced disorder.

The paths to substance-related disorders and the variety of substances used are diverse. Courtney's story shows that psychiatric drugs are not always the answer. Psychiatric medication can often be used successfully during treatment, however, as it was in Pierre's case.

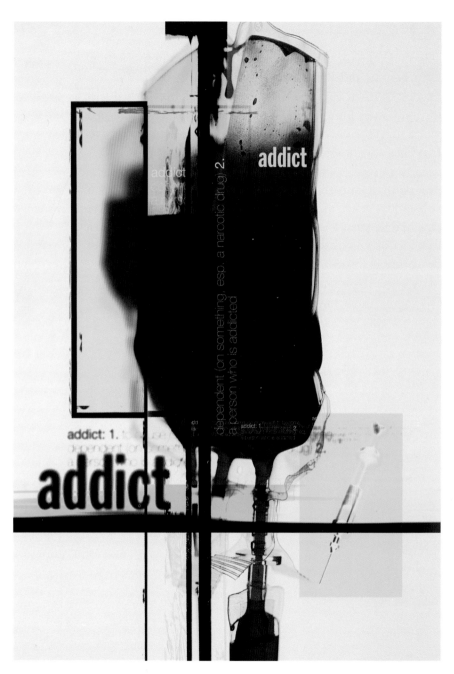

Psychiatric drugs do not offer a simple solution to people with an addiction. These medications are also chemicals, and they have their own risks and side effects.

6 | Risks and Side Effects

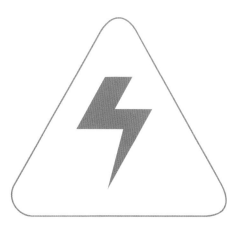

When physicians prescribe medication, they expect it to cause specific beneficial effects that will help treat the patient's condition. Side effects are additional and usually **adverse** symptoms that can also occur in the body as a result of taking a medication. Side effects vary from one person to the next. They may not occur at all, they may be minimal and mild, or they can be severe and even dangerous. A physician can rarely determine ahead of time which side effects might affect a specific individual. As with almost all prescribed medications, some side effects are possible when beginning a treatment program that includes the use of psychiatric medications.

ANTABUSE

GLOSSARY

adverse: Harmful.

Side effects are not common when using Antabuse, but some individuals will experience them. If a bad taste in the

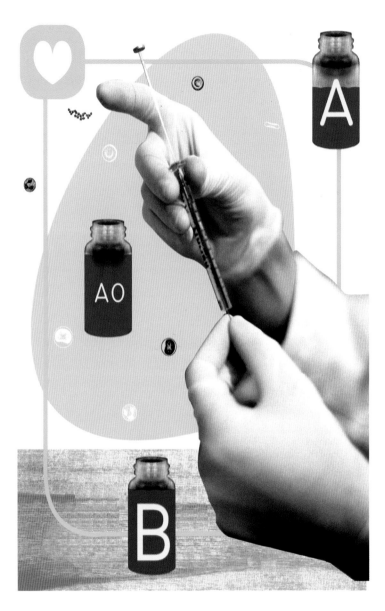

Any chemical that enters your bloodstream will have a variety of effects on your body.

mouth, a headache, sleepiness, or ***impotence*** occurs, these symptoms will usually be temporary, disappearing within a couple of weeks without additional treatment. If they remain, it may be necessary to reduce the Antabuse dose. Any skin rashes that develop can be treated with an ***antihistamine***. Hepatitis or other liver problems, psychosis, or neuritis (a painful inflammation of the nerves) are side effects that rarely develop, but if they do, they call for discontinuance of the medication.

GLOSSARY

impotence: For males, the inability to have sex. This is sometimes a side effect of medication.

antihistamine: Compounds that are used to combat allergic reactions.

NALTREXONE

Possible side effects of naltrexone use include chills, dizziness, both diarrhea and constipation, headaches, fatigue, anxiety, nausea and vomiting, impotence, pain in the muscles and joints, rashes, decreased appetite and increased thirst, and both insomnia and sleeplessness. Most individuals taking naltrexone for maintenance after treatment for alcohol addiction do not experience these side effects, however, and they are usually temporary in the individuals who do have them. As long as the person in treatment does not experience liver problems, the medication can be taken indefinitely. Naltrexone is not an addictive substance, so it does not have potential for abuse, and withdrawal symptoms do not occur with discontinued use.

NICOTINE

Since nicotine is an extremely addictive substance, cessation of smoking behavior is a challenging undertaking for individuals with this substance-related disorder. Most individuals do not succeed on their first attempt to conquer this chemical.

Nicotine patches, especially when used in combination with behavioral therapy, have helped many individuals succeed, however. Skin irritation is a common side effect when using nicotine patches as treatment for an addiction to cigarettes, but simply moving the placement spot for the patches to different areas of the body usually solves this problem. Other side effects, including nausea, dizziness, and both insomnia and vivid dreams, are much less common, are not generally cause for concern, and usually disappear after a short time.

Several side effects occur commonly when using nicotine gum, including nausea, vomiting, and stomachache along with dizziness, hiccups, aching jaw, and sore mouth and throat. Less common are loss of appetite, headache, insomnia, and an increase in saliva. Chewing the gum more slowly and periodically holding it in the mouth without chewing can reduce side effects.

METHADONE

Possible side effects when beginning a methadone-maintenance program include sweating, lightheadedness and dizziness, sedation, nausea, and vomiting. These symptoms are usually minor, however, and generally disappear with continued use of the medication. It is usually only individuals with preexisting health conditions who develop more serious side effects, such as heart or respiratory problems. Conditions like these can mandate a reduced dose of the medication or even discontinuing the program. The only frequently reported complication of methadone use is constipation, which can be easily remedied with the use of a laxative.

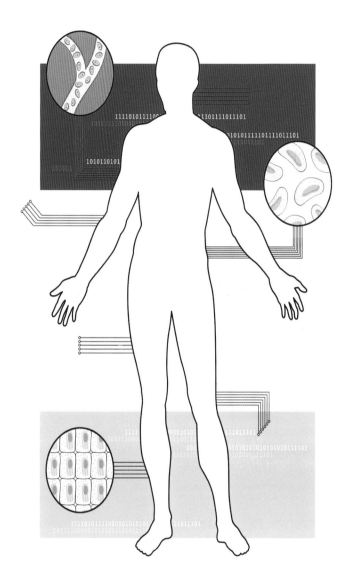

When a chemical enters your bloodstream, it may cause a variety of reactions elsewhere in your body.

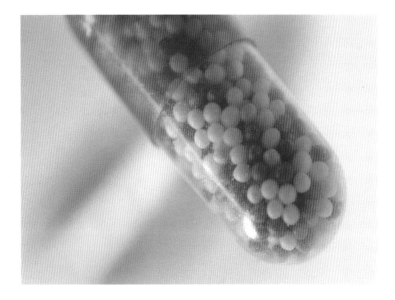

The same drug may be prescribed for a variety of reasons.

CLONIDINE

Common side effects of clonidine use include dry mouth, drowsiness, and sedation. Clonidine is often prescribed to lower blood pressure in patients with high blood pressure without a substance-related disorder. Therefore, the blood pressure of individuals using clonidine as part of a treatment program for a substance-related disorder should be monitored. If it falls too low, lightheadedness and dizziness may result. Since this could result in a fall, elderly individuals using this medication for any reason should be closely monitored. Other side effects are rare but include weakness, rashes, nausea, and vomiting. If negative symptoms occur, the dose should be lowered.

BUPRENORPHINE

Reported side effects during tests involving buprenorphine include diarrhea, insomnia, and increased sweating. Individuals may experience some withdrawal symptoms after using buprenorphine, although they are less severe than those caused by methadone withdrawal.

BENZODIAZEPINES

Since their introduction in the 1960s there has been debate about the addictive qualities of benzodiazepines. The potential for abuse exists with the availability of any addictive substance and increases with the extended use of the substance over a long period of time. Physicians are aware of

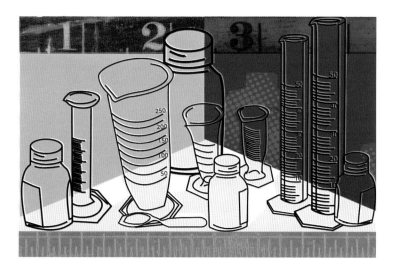

A pharmacist measures each prescription exactly. The patient should always exactly follow dosing instructions as well.

Sometimes the treatment for a substance-related disorder can also be addictive. Caution should always be used when taking a benzodiazepine.

Drinking and driving is dangerous—but so is driving when under the influence of a benzodiazepine.

this and take it into account when using this medication for treatment of alcohol addiction.

Aside from the potential for addiction, side effects are minimal. The individual may become sleepier, but this is not considered a negative symptom. In fact, it may be desirable during withdrawal. Sometimes the dose is decreased or more time is allowed to elapse between doses to reduce sleepiness.

Sometimes the drug Librium is administered intravenously to individuals who are hospitalized during alcohol withdrawal. Hospital staff are present to monitor the patient's vital signs during this procedure. Although it is not common, some individuals have experienced decreased breathing (and in rare cases, stopped breathing) when Librium was administered in this manner. If this should hap-

pen, oxygen is given to the patient until he begins breathing again on his own.

BUPROPION

Some individuals can experience seizures if bupropion (Wellbutrin and Zyban) is administered to them at certain levels, so the dosage is closely regulated. More common side effects include restlessness, insomnia, agitation, weight loss, and anxiety. Some individuals taking Wellbutrin have experienced confusion, hallucinations, delusions, and paranoia.

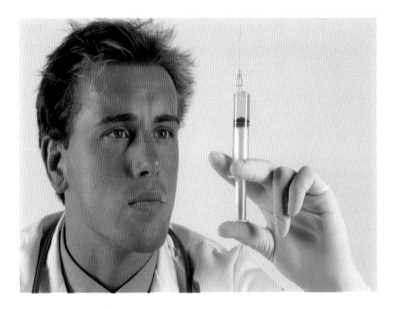

Some kinds of drug treatment for addiction need to be monitored by hospital staff.

A person taking any medication should immediately report unusual or uncomfortable symptoms to her physician. The physician will then decide if the dose of the medication being administered should be reduced or completely stopped. The physician may want to substitute another medication or prescribe an additional medication to treat the unpleasant side effect being experienced.

A person who is addicted to cocaine is suffering from a mental, emotional, and physical condition.

7 | Alternative and Supplementary Treatments

Some treatments for substance-related disorders are more commonly used than others. The most successful treatments often combine the use of psychiatric medication with psychotherapy. People with substance-related disorders are suffering from a mental, emotional, and physical condition. Though drugs can be helpful in treatment, it is unlikely that they alone will break the pattern of substance addiction. The individual has a better chance at complete recovery if medications are combined with counseling or membership and participation in a recovery program.

Everything we see and do, even talking, has the power to affect our brain. Talking to a therapist or members of a self-help group can be a very powerful form of treatment for a substance-related disorder.

Cognitive-behavioral therapy, which incorporates training in social and coping skills, is among the most successful. The social-skills component of a program such as this may involve assertiveness training under the direction of a pro-

GLOSSARY

confrontational: Having to do with face-to-face conflict.

empathy: The awareness and understanding of the feelings of someone else.

fessional. The individual's communication skills might also be further developed. The goal is for the person to be better able to express herself and to interact appropriately in various situations. These skills can reduce a person's anxiety and struggle in daily life and may make it easier for her to avoid the temptation to use a mind-altering substance to obtain relief from the stresses of life.

Family therapy is also useful in dealing with substance-related disorders, as the family needs to know how to help the individual in crisis and how to keep the family unit healthy and together.

The approach of the therapist may have a great deal to do with the success or failure of some individuals in dealing with their substance-related disorder. Certain traditional approaches are *confrontational*, and many people do not react well to this approach. Some evidence suggests that therapists who demonstrate more encouragement and *empathy* toward their clients may have more overall success in helping individuals conquer addiction. One successful method that uses this approach is called motivational-enhancement therapy.

Many individuals with anxiety or depression find relief through meditation and relaxation techniques. There are several ways to do this; deep, abdominal breathing is a component of many of them. While you breathe deeply, try to clear your mind of all thoughts and to calm and relax your body. With mindful meditation, a person allows thoughts to float through his mind, while he remains detached. Progressive relaxation techniques call for the individual to systematically tighten and then relax muscles. Typically one tenses and then relaxes specific parts of the body, working from one end of the body to the other, until the entire body has been relaxed. Gentle stretching, deep breathing, and mind-soothing exercise like that found in yoga can be very beneficial in reducing both anxiety and depression.

Meditation is one way to cope with tension and depression without using drugs. Many self-help books, tapes, and classes are available to teach meditation techniques.

GLOSSARY

acupuncture: An ancient Chinese treatment that involves puncturing the body with needles at specific points to relieve pain and treat disease.

Some people report that ***acupuncture*** has helped to reduce their cravings for specific substances. It has been used successfully to treat cravings in individuals addicted to cocaine.

Probably the most well known treatment for substance abuse in North America is that conducted by Alcoholics Anonymous, often referred to as AA. Alcoholics Anonymous offers a self-directed program that includes group support provided by individuals who are in recovery from this substance-related disorder. Alcoholics Anonymous does not advocate the use of any psychiatric medications as part of treatment for substance-related disorders. Instead, it relies on a twelve-step program, and the recovering members of the group who reach out to others and help them by sharing their own experience. The treatment is called a twelve-step program because participants study, then usually accept and model their lives after, the twelve steps that were writ-

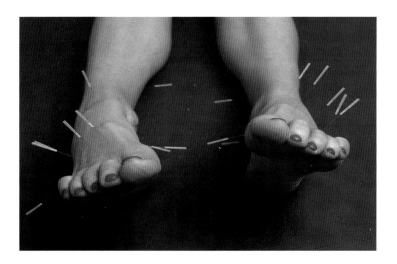

Acupuncture may be an effective alternative treatment for addiction.

The Twelve Steps of Alcoholics Anonymous

1. We admitted we were powerless over alcohol—that our lives had become unmanageable.
2. Came to believe that a Power greater than ourselves could restore us to sanity.
3. Made a decision to turn our will and our lives over to the care of God as we understood Him.
4. Made a searching and fearless moral inventory of ourselves.
5. Admitted to God, to ourselves, and to another human being the exact nature of our wrongs.
6. Were entirely ready to have God remove all these defects of character.
7. Humbly asked Him to remove our shortcomings.
8. Made a list of all persons we had harmed, and became willing to make amends to them all.
9. Made direct amends to such people wherever possible, except when to do so would injure them or others.
10. Continued to take personal inventory and when we were wrong promptly admitted it.
11. Sought through prayer and meditation to improve our conscious contact with God as we understood Him, praying only for knowledge of His will for us and the power to carry that out.
12. Having had a spiritual awakening as the result of these steps, we tried to carry this message to alcoholics and to practice these principles in all our affairs.

ten by the earliest members of AA to describe how they are recovering. Individuals who are interested in becoming associated with Alcoholics Anonymous but do not feel they can believe in or adhere to the twelve steps are not required to do so. Instead, they are asked to read AA literature,

Natural remedies have not been approved by the FDA. Although they come from natural substances, they contain chemicals, just like any other drug, and they should be used with caution.

attend meetings regularly, and keep an open mind about the twelve steps. There are many twelve-step programs modeled after AA, including Narcotics Anonymous, Cocaine Anonymous, and so on.

Alternative remedies for substance abuse disorders may also include herbs, vitamins, and dietary supplements, some of which have been used for centuries by peoples around the world. Caution should be used when taking these substances. The U.S. Food and Drug Administration regulates the prescription drugs used by psychiatrists and other doctors for the treatment of psychiatric disorders, which means that these drugs must pass a rigorous series of trials before they can be advertised and claims can be made for their effectiveness. No such rigorous demands exist for herbs, vitamins, and dietary supplements.

According to the American Psychiatric Association, substance-related disorders are the main cause of preventable illness and premature death in the United States. Whether an individual is in the initial stages of a substance-related disorder, has entered into full-blown addiction, is experiencing withdrawal, or is in recovery, the support of family and friends, of a self-help group, and of counseling can be extremely important to successful initial and long-term treatment.

GLOSSARY

stigma: An identifying mark or characteristic with negative connotations.

If you know someone with a substance-related disorder, have compassion for him. The social *stigma* associated with substance-related disorders can be very difficult for anyone to bear. If you think you may be at risk for developing a substance-related disorder, discuss your concerns with your parents, a trusted teacher, your family physician, or a counselor. If you are already using one of the substances that can cause a disorder, try to discontinue use. If you are unable to do so, the disorder already exists, and you need to seek immediate advice in dealing with the situation.

Help is available to assist you with this condition. What's more, obtaining assistance to rid yourself of the substance-related disorder can save your life.

FURTHER READING

Babbit, Nikki. *Adolescent Drug & Alcohol Abuse: How to Spot It, Stop It, and Get Help for Your Family*. San Francisco: O'Reilly, 2000.

Burgess, Melvin. *Smack*. New York: Avon, 1999.

Davenport-Hines, Richard. *The Pursuit of Oblivion: A Global History of Narcotics*. New York: Norton, 2002.

Gorman, Jack M. *The Essential Guide to Psychiatric Drugs*. New York: St Martin's, 1997.

Rustin, Terry A. *Quit & Stay Quit: A Personal Program to Stop Smoking*. Center City, Minn.: Hazeldon, 1994.

Volpicelli, Joseph, and Maia Szalavitz. *Recovery Options: The Complete Guide*. New York: John Wiley & Sons, 2000.

Wechsler, Henry, and Bernice Wuethrich. *Dying to Drink: Confronting Binge Drinking on College Campuses*. Emmaus, Pa.: Rodale. 2002.

FOR MORE INFORMATION

Connecticut Clearinghouse
www.ctclearinghouse.org

The Food and Drug Administration
www.fda.gov

The National Clearing House for Alcohol and Drug Information
www.health.org/newsroom/

National Institute on Drug Abuse
www.drugabuse.gov

Recovery Story Page
www.addictions.org/stories.htm

Publisher's Note:

The Web sites listed on this page were active at the time of publication. The publisher is not responsible for Web sites that have changed their address or discontinued operation since the date of publication. The publisher will review and update the Web sites upon each reprint.

INDEX

BIOGRAPHIES

Joyce Libal is a graduate of the University of Wisconsin. She lives in northeastern Pennsylvania where she works as a magazine editor and freelance writer.

Mary Ann Johnson is a licensed child and adolescent clinical nurse specialist and a family psychiatric nurse practitioner in the state of Massachusetts. She completed her psychotherapy training at Cambridge Hospital and her psychopharmacology training at Massachusetts General Hospital. She is the director of clinical trials in the pediatric psychopharmacology research unit at Massachusetts General Hospital.

Donald Esherick has spent seventeen years working in the pharmaceutical industry and is currently an associate director of Worldwide Regulatory Affairs with Wyeth Research in Philadelphia, Pennsylvania. He specializes in the chemistry section (manufacture and testing) of investigational and marketed drugs.